I Mash Potatoes On My Face, What You Do Today?

By
Irish Brian Kelly
Poet, Engineer, Landscaper, Lover

I Mash Potatoes On My Face, What You Do Today?

Written By Irish Brian Kelly
Published By Andy Whorehall and Life Artners
Transcribed, Edited, Created By Dave DeCastris and Andy Whorehall
Cover Artwork By Jesus Correa
Art Direction, Design, Layout By Andy Whorehall and Dave DeCastris
Additional Irish Bullshit By Bono, Edge, Larry, Adam, Saint Paladius
Executive Producers: Lord Thomas Derby and Johnny Emerald The IIIrd
Forewords By Jesus Correa, Eric Knoll, Jason "Mossy" Vaughn, Andy Whorehall, Dave DeCastris, Uncle Liam Kelly, Aunt Mammy Kelly, Lorenzo Bottums, Barkley, Sparky, Winslow, Gordon, Jay, Mark

Thank Yous to Jesus Correa, Eric Knoll, and Jason "Mossy" Vaughn for their last minute creative contributions. May the three of you always be childlike and evergreen. Not leprechaun green. Childlike and evergreen– very rare qualities. Honored to know each of you for extremely different, influential reasons. You make this potato-peelin' way of life worth working, writing, and sketching through when the dull, dark, domestic ways of adulthood responsibilities and daytime blues come around– and they do moreso than I need them to. I don't have much to say to everyone else here as it's all in this book. Let me save you the time if reading isn't your thing: I think you're all a sack of potatoes, selfish and driven by material goals, wants–not needs, and full of shit. Yep. Potatoes mashed on your face, every page.

Copyright © 2015 Andy Whorehall, Under Exclusive License With Life Artners Publishing. Reproduction not permitted. Taking photos of content, words, and images contained within this book to share and litter as useless data on the internet is OK as long as you use hashtags titled "*POTATOES*," "*IRISHBRIAN*," "*YOU$A*™," and "*andywhorehall*." All rights reserved.

FIRST EDITION
ISBN-13: 978-0692554616
ISBN-10: 0692554610

Irish Brian Kelly: Poet, Engineer, Landscaper, Lover

Dedication

Dear Bono, Edge, Larry, Adam,
Lord Thomas Derby, Saint Palladius,
Katie and Otis:

I'm a street with no name without all of you.

You taught me to be whoever I wish to be,

and so it is– I am Irish Brian Kelly:

Poet, Engineer, Landscaper, and Lover.

Like Palladius before me, I am no saint nor irishman, my Otis.

Alas:

Snakes Need A Severance, Potatoes Need A Peelin, Faces Need A Mashin'

Soups Need A Stirrin, Breads Need A Bakin, Ponies Need A Pokin'!

Potatoes Need A Peelin':

Jay, Gordon, Mark, Heather, Kneemon and Sparky Need A Spankin'

Quarry Shazzelle, Tim and Frank Shear, Too.

POTATOES!

(LOL = #LaughsOutLouds = EL OH EL+ hahahaha.)

and so it is once more with why I've become Irish Brian Kelly:

Poet, Engineer, Landscaper, and Lover;

an Adopted Son of Dublin,

via Belvidere of Illinois,

in the United States of America.

To you, my readers, Irish or not:

Together we can go where the streets have no names with this book and give them names: European, American, Chinese, anything– HTML, PHP, Hashtags and any language you want to be with your new name to populate the internets with more of nothing. That's right– YOU$A!™

GO GO GO, BONO, GOALLLLOL!

Irish Brian Kelly, October 10th, 2015

Forewords

Crushed Doritos On Our Gym Teachers Chests
By Jesus Correa

Hello.
This is my introduction to your book, Irish Brian Kelly.
As you, already, you already are aware that I am a gullible moron,
or I would not be here.
Milky.
Creamy.
Lumpy buttery clumps .
Mashed. In your face.
A lot of talk of Bono.
Smashed in your face.
Hello.
I am a former mayoral candidate from–and for–Rockford, Illinois.
Thanks.
I read a good portion of this book on my hand me down iPhone.
I was given this iPhone as a gift.
I am writing the introduction to this book on the blood, sweat, and tears of ling dead Chinese woman.
Thank you, future.
How does it–or do it–feel to have the mashing of potatoes on your face?
I came in four out of a four-to-four race.
My mother disgraced.
Dead peopel will always stay dead, and I will always be mediocre.
I cannot tell if I am embarrassed by this travesty or if this tragedy should be embarrassed by me.
Irish Brian Kelly don't give no fuck about what you think.
Great.
Makes me want to kick morons in the throat again in a joyous manner.
Makes me want to have a long slap-me-in-the-face contest in the mirror again.
Should I be pissed off?
Am I really a moron?

Irish Brian Kelly: *Poet, Engineer, Landscaper, Lover*

I enjoyed the confusion.
Like being spun around in grade school on a tire swing by a kid named Lionel,
Lionel with a renewed death wish.
In closing, and without a dew,
Brian Kelly is going to mash potato in your face.
You are going to enjoy it whether you want to or not.
You are going to feel like a moron and a coward, as you should.
Brian Kelly is going to mash these ugly, mean, tender, soft, awkward potatoes in your face if you like it or not.
I like it. Thumbs up. Lola g.
P.s.: All of your tupperware is ill-gotten.
Your patio set makes me nauseous.
Let us all crush Doritos on our gym teachers chests.

– Jesus Correa, October 17th, 2015

Jesus Correa © Photo by Breanda Fedie

I Mash Potatoes On My Face, What You Do Today?

Stairway To The Potatoes
By Jason Mossy Vaughn

A book foreword is a stupid marketing tool. Potential purchasers of the book may read the first page or so of the foreword, right after they read the shit on the back , and–the author hopes–right before they buy the book. What you say in a book's forward matters, and I am supposed to write a forward for my friend Brian Kelly… "Polish this turd," is what he said.

There's a potato who's sure all that glitters is gold
And he is buying a stairway to potato
When he gets there he knows, if the stores are all closed
With a word he can get what he came for potatoes
Ooh, ooh, and he's buying a stairway to potato

There's a sign on the wall but he wants to be sure
'Cause you know sometimes potatoes have two meanings
In a tree by the brook, there's a potato who sings
Sometimes all of our thoughts are misgiven
Ooh, it makes me wonder about potatoes
Ooh, it makes me wonder about potatoes

There's a feeling I get when I look to the potato
And my spirit is crying for mashed face potatoes
In my thoughts I have seen potatoes smoking through the trees
And the voices of potatoes who stand looking
Ooh, it makes me wonder about potatoes
Ooh, it really makes me wonder about potatoes

And it's whispered that soon if we all call the potato
Then the piper will lead us to mashed potato mountain
And a new day will dawn for those who mash potato in your face
And the forests will echo with potatoes
If there's a bustle in your potato, don't be alarmed now

Irish Brian Kelly: *Poet, Engineer, Landscaper, Lover*

It's just a spring clean for the May Potato
Yes, there are two paths you can go by, but in the long run
There's still time to change the potato you're on
And it makes me wonder about potatoes

Your head is humming and it won't go, in case you don't know
The potato is calling you to join him
Dear lady, can you hear the wind blow and did you know
Your stairway lies on the mashed potato

– Jason Mossy Vaughn, October 14th, 2015

Jason "Mossy" Vaughn © Photo by Dana Vaughn

A Moving Foreword
By Jojowrinkles

I first met Brian Kelly in 1986, just outside of Zurich, Switzerland. Minding my own business is my business, but I heard a poet, an artist if you will, whispering to me, literally. I didn't know him then, but Brian had walked over to my table where I was casually eating Azeitao, my favorite Portuguese sheep's milk cheese (produced near Lisbon). Noticing my unusual taste and uncanny ability to ignore everyone and everything around me, IBK, as I came to know him, ever so softly repeated this word–"jojowrinkles"–to me, almost like a lullaby. Brian then pinched my ear, picked up the cheese, which at this point was runny and sublime in flavor, texture, and appearance, and deftly using his thumb and forefinger as a weapon, smashed it into my ear.

A friendship was born.

Jojowrinkles became my moniker and Brian became my sage and my champion. He introduced me to numerous limericks referencing things such as the jaw harp, Stephen Dedalus, gourmet macaroni and cheese, and early-20th century Andorran handguns, among others. I breathed in his relentless pursuit of a world in which he could become a Bonofide (his term) legend, leaving traces of his genius for his brothers and sisters in all corners of the universe, but only a universe centered in Africa, northeast Sri Lanka, and Ketchum, Idaho. As I became a renowned master of interpreting James Brown's post-1969/pre-1977 soul output on my Fisher Price harmonica, so too did Brian begin his obsession with expanding on Olatunji's "Drums of Passion" cycle on his piccolo with a focus on one day realizing his dream of creating an Irish-themed tribute for sound and stage in honor of the late, great Brian Piccolo. While that project has not come to fruition, I know that Brian would love for all people to be aware of this project.

Brian saw in me a zest for cantankerous, malicious intent towards all of the things that the Kreator created. He saw it in me because he saw it in himself and all of the people around him. He peers into souls the way Coca Cola burns battery acid - with a searing intensity.

This is his work. This is his art. Embrace it. Embrace yourself. Embrace your neighbors and their animals. Embrace people that walk in his shadow and His shadow. Brian wants you to walk in the light. Brian wants it to be this way, because Brian is God.

– *Jojowrinkles, October 17, 2015*

Eric Jojowrinkles Knoll © Photo by Kathy Knoll

She Wore Lemon, Not Potato
By Andy Whorehall

The first time I met Brian, I knew he was Irish. Not in a lucky way, but in a special, all-caps locked, celtic way. He played for the opposing Shuffleboard team at Mulligan's Bar In Rockford, IL. My teammate, Dan Yurek, said to me, "Check out this fucking quack," and I did.

I didn't know what to think at first. He kept interrupting matches by rushing over to the jukebox to play a steady stream of U2 songs. Every team that his played against won because of the constant distractions and terrible jukebox takeover– except mine.

Dan and I destroyed Irish Brian and his teammate, Uncle Liam, 15-1. Irish Brian yelled, "REMATCH, MOTHER FUCKER." We obliged, and we lost the next game 15-13. Brian did something different during that rematch: He didn't interrupt the game to play awful U2 songs on the jukebox. He was smarter than that. Mr. Kelly and his uncle had paid for the song, "Lemon," by U2, to be played on repeat. The entire rematch and every game afterwards went down to the same song. It got to me, it got to my teammate.

We were so distraught by Irish Brian's Shuffleboard tactics that we lost it. Dan and I picked up our pucks and threw them at Mr. Kelly and his uncle. Brian laughed at me and said, "YOU THROW PUCK ONE MORE TIME I MASH TATOE ON YOUR FACE, WOP!" I started laughing immediately. We all laughed. The entire bar laughed.

Andy Whorehall © Photo by Katie Maringer

I shook his hand and said, "You're a goddamn poet, Irish Brian!" And then he mashed a potato on my fucking face. True story.

Irish Brian and I have been Shuffleboard friends and internet enemies since. It's my pleasure to help him publish his first book by transcribing his thoughts from bar napkins to this. Whatever this is.

– Andy Whorehall, October 17th, 2015

"I PLAY U2 SONG SHE WORE LEMON TWENTY-EIGHT TIMES IN A ROW TO PLAY SHUFFLEBOARD THAT IS HOW I MENTALLY DEFEAT AMERICANS AND THEN YOU AND THAT OTHER TALL MOTHER FUCKER YOU PLAY SHUFFLEBOARD WITH SNAP AFTER SHE WORE LEMON FIVE TIMES. YOU STUPID AMERICANS THROW PUCKS AT ME AND UNCLE LIAM AND MISS BECAUSE YOU THROW SPORTS BALL LIKE DRUNK MOMMY DOS ON WEEKEND BENDER. SO I RUN BEHIND BAR AND GRAB IRISH POTATOES. I MASH MULLIGAN TATOES ON YOUR FACE. SHE WORE LEMON PLAY TWENTY-THREE MORE TIMES. I WIN SHUFFLEBOARD! HAHA. IF YOU READ THIS AND SAY WTF HE SAY?! I SAY SO WHAT." *– Irish Brian Kelly*

I Mash Potatoes On My Face, What You Do Today?

Totem Polems
&
Totaled Poelems
Po'Tatoes
&
Tatoes

Irish Brian Kelly: *Poet, Engineer, Landscaper, Lover*

I AM BRIAN KELLY AND I AM IRISH, ARE YOU? HaHaHa!

I STARTED AN IRISH INTERNET BLOG BECAUSE I WAS TIRED OF MY FRIENDS BEATING ME UP EVERY TIME I TOLD THEM, "*I'M GOING TO BE A WRITER.*"

I'M FROM BELVIDERE, IL, AND I WORK IN CHICAGO BY DAY AS AN ENGINEER. I SPEND MOST OF MY DAYS THINKING OF POEMS, WORDS, PHRASES, BEER, POTATOES, AND SENTENCES TO WRITE ABOUT INSTEAD OF FIXING DRAWBRIDGE DESIGNS AND INNER CITY ROUND ABOUTS FOR POOR AMERICAN CITIES LIKE ROCKFORD, IL. LOL.

I PUT ON LOTS OF MUSIC BY BONO AND DAVID GRAY AT NIGHT, AND THEN I TRANSCRIBE IRISH THOUGHTS FROM PAGES OF NOTEPAD SCRIBBLES TO IRISH INTERNET WORDS AT IRISHBRIAN.COM.

DUE TO MY SHELTERED UPBRINGING IN BELVIDERE, IL, I BECAME CONSUMED WITH THE CELTIC CULTURE. PLEASE DON'T HOLD IT AGAINST ME IF I CASUALLY YELL OUT "GO GO GO, *BONO!*" IN MY ARTICLES AND POEMS.

MOVING TO CHICAGO AFTER COLLEGE HELPED ME EXPAND MY AMERICAN TASTES, BUT I ALWAYS COME BACK TO U2'S "*ACHTUNG BABY!*". HAHAHA, WHAT A WONDERFUL IRISH POP RECORD WITH A HALF GERMAN TITLE.

I HOPE YOU ENJOY MY TOTEM POLEMS AND TOTALED POELEMS. THEY MIGHT NOT BE AS BORING AS SOME OF MY FELLOW IRISHMEN'S BOOK OF POEMS, BUT THEY'LL DEFINITELY BE AS SATISFYING AS A TALL MUG OF GREEN MILLER LITE OR BUD LIGHT IN THE MONTH OF MARCH IN AMERICA. LOL– FOOLS! ST. PATTY WASN'T IRISH!
LISTEN UP WHEN YOU NEED ME, BABY, YOU CAN HEAR MY FRANDS CHANT AFTER 8 PINTS OF GUINNESS, "*FIGHT FIGHT FIGHT, BRIAN, FIGHT!*" NO! I WON'T FIGHT NO MORE! I WILL WRITE! FOR YOU AND MY HOMELAND. I WILL WRITE, FOR I AM IRISH BRIAN KELLY!

GO GO GO, BONO, GO!

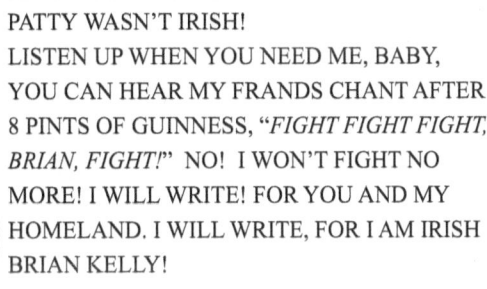

Drunks

People, sharks
Doggie barks
Singularly plural
Out of oatmeal
Again?
Daddy left the newspaper on the kitchen table
A bruise on mommy's face
Transmissions interfered
Cracked land below
Waters, dark
Mermaids
Stop

Bye bye, earth.

Below the cracked ocean floor
Transmissions interfered
Sharks above circle on standby
Listen for laughing
"Mermaids, stop"
You can hear them whispering
Radios
Long lost and drowned
Gargle in unison
With matching cards that read
"Bye, bye, Earth"
I like it here
No one leaves
No one talks
No one cares
Everything above is clearer now
Below the cracked ocean floor

Folk Hue!

Folk hue, Roquefort!
Folk hue, won time!
Folk hue, four thymes!
Folk hue, mister meerasake!
Folk hue, jay jay pony!
Folk hue, gordon buttons!
Folk hue, sparky pony!
Folk hue, heether hor!
Folk hue, cheap truck!
Folk hue, francis shears!
Folk hue, pot holes!
#lol
Folk hue, Roquefort!

We The People Drown

We sat and waited for balloons to pop
We sat and listened to the train talk
We sat and watched the people drown
We listened to Bono sing on the radio
"I still haven't found what I'm looking for"
Fuck your town
We're outta here

Sea Horse

You are
"No, you are"
No, you are!
"Uh, no. You are"
No, you're a sea horse!
"No, no, and NO!
You're a sea horse!"
Ok

Transcendental Molars

Brigades of blue
the crust of dry wax
once lit and melted
soaked the paper plate we ate our frozen pizza off of last night
her body boiled
the scent, a bartender's last call hovered like a cloud above the duvet
it, stitched together from the colors of my country,
green, white, and orange slightly covered her news anchor-orange-skin
she awoke asking of bacon and the pig,
but we'd eaten the last of the lot
we talked of the revolution
druids, damien rice, and bono
breakfast, spaceships, and teeth
She said I had nice teeth and a soft tongue
I said, "Thanks. Your orange ass looked nice on top of my green duvet."

I wish I could remember her name.

Cousin Jonny Was A Race Car Driver

Cousin Jonny was a race car driver
From the green fields of Waterford, Ireland
to the south of Belvidere, Illinois
Cousin Jonny never learned to swim
You can still here him 20 miles out
Spitting up grain and gravel
Chasing chicks and breaking hearts
Irish Cousin Jonny rarely raced to lose his monies
Silver rims stole green bills from other drivers' egos
They who dared and never conquered
Roads the natives couldn't master
The coolest cousin I never met sent his monies home
Across the border from Kilkenny
To aunts and uncles never met
He never raced for wealth and women
And as easy they came to Cousin Jonny
They always came and went
Some never came again

Cousin Jonny was a race car driver, the proudest son of Waterford and Belvidere, who drove his car hood first into the Rock River on his way to conquer Rockford.

Irish Brian Kelly: *Poet, Engineer, Landscaper, Lover*

Big Pants

Big pants
Store away for a fat day
No need to return
Don't give away
Or exchange

Big pants can be stored away for a fat day.

5 Year Warranty

Counter top, counter top.
Sitting chair and drinking pop.
Building buddy builds a pyramid for a big ol' bonfire!
What a bore.
Bring your papers, bring it all.
Drop it off, pile it up, and watch it burn-
or craft a counter top!

Counter top, oh counter top.
Looking tough, now giving up.
Building buddy builds a pyramid out of paper, gasoline, and empty beer cans.

We laughed at you, counter top.
We laughed at you too, paper!
We laughed at the pile, a pyramid pattern set afire.

Counter top, oh counter top.
We didn't mean to burn you!
You were a good counter top.

Don't be mad, counter top, you came with a five year warranty.

Counter top, oh counter top.
You are happy again!

Smell Them Sleeping

Fire on the mountain

Lighting up your dreams

Waking wolves from their sleep

"Mmm, mm, mmmmmm" howl the coyotes

Bears on standby sharpening their teeth

Searching for a family

An American one

Large and proud

White and loud

So fat, so delicious

You can smell them sleeping, simmering for miles

There are thousands of organisms to eat

Crucified For Flavors

Rocks crushed

Remnants resurrected revealed flapjacks three days later

Buttered pools of maple bacon manufactured steam from sausage links

Plastic plates serving up space ship saunas

Torn napkins wrapping heads like gas masks

A last supper

Breakfast before we hit the banks

Four days ago we hung the pigs

Crucified

Favors for flavors

Frogs In The Henhouse

Frogs in the henhouse are still frogs in the henhouse, but lost
"Ribbit, ribbit" fills the farm all night long
Hens awaking chickens call out,
"Cukoo ca-choo, cuh-cukoo ca-choo!"
The farmer's wife is angry, sleepless, selfish, and unsatisfied
"Can you please kill those froggies, honey?"
Farmer Ronnie catches a frog, but feels guilty and sets him free
3 years passed and the little chickens, once hens, are now chanting
"Ribbit, ribbit!" all night long
The farmer's wife has had enough
You could hear her all day long going
"Cukoo ca choo, cuh-cukoo ca-choo!"
And then one day there was nothing

Farmer Ronnie was a nice man to the animals
His wife stabbed him 14 times
and drowned him in the pond next to the farm
The frogs in the henhouse are not frogs in the henhouse anymore

Bubba, Jalen Rose

Fab 5 rebel
So mean, Jalen
Bubba, you so mean!

Duke hatin'
'Uncle Tom' statin'
Bubba, you Fab 5 rebel!

Jalen Rose
From the west side of Detroit
You were 17
Bubba, I forgive you!

This is all so weird, Jalen
My Uncle's name is Tom, too
Bubba, I forgive you!

Big Balls Fell

Big balls sat bloated behind barbed wire
Big green, orange, and white balls
mixed between reds and baby blues
sat trapped, constipated by a cage
in a corporate supermarket
Standing between breakfast cereals
and bags of Mexican corn tortilla chips
my country's balls spoke to me
"Damn thee red, and damn thee baby blue balls!
Free the greens, son
free the oranges, brotha
and free the whites, but lastly
March onward, Brian, onward
For Ireland!"
Revolutions begin and end in larger supermarkets
Big balls fell

I Mash Potatoes On My Face, What You Do Today?

Saint Bono's Day
March 16th

GO GO GO,

Bono,

GO!

FIGHT FIGHT FIGHT,

Bono,

FIGHT!

For POTATOES!

For POVERTY!

For POPES!

For PRESIDENTS!

For TRAINS!

For ROCKFORD! lol

For IRELAND!

It is you, Bono, it is YOU that WE, earth's peasants, PRAY TO?

YES YES YES, it is you, BONO!

NOT PATRICK- YOU!

GO GO GO,

BONO,

GOALLLLLLLLL!

Joie De Vivre, I Forgive your Fans

Jerry Martin, 8 minutes ago said,
"I'm bummed I didn't get the LP the other day."

Band Page admin announced,
"free run, forgive us if we act a foo"

Marcus Nuccio likes this

Wyatt Overman can guarantee who won't be acting a foo

Pizzah Partie said,
"That could be the title of an amateur youtube parkour video"

Me, I'm like what is up and LOL, OMG!

Band Page admin announced again,
"free rum, forgive us"

4 hours ago
Like, Unlike
View Feedback, Hide Feedback
2 people like this

Joie De Vivre, I forgive your fans.

Big Pants (Part Two)

Big pants,
it's been awhile
since I've seen you.

There was no need to return you,
give away, or exchange;
but how long can I store you away for a fat day?

Big pants,
I'm really sorry I lost that much weight.
Don't cry, big pants.

I'll get back to you soon.

Feast For A King

Surfing through the blackout;
eating snacks a couch can't hold-
a troubled man's condition.

How they'd never believe you
about that one time you had a plan.
An Elvis-like pursuit.

How they'd never believe you
as it comes off like a joke.
How much crap defines a man when you shove it down his throat?

They can hear it in your breath.
Mr. Fridge is filled with fat;
the freezer's filled with death.

Flying whale laughed!
"No man knows the power of a heart's attack,"
the silly fish happily said.

They didn't believe you, again, when you told them he died there with his
stool and a half-eaten hot peanut butter and banana sandwich,
fried.

Feast for a king!

Balloons Tied To Tailpipes

My body made a boat with two doors afloat.
Green Buick, I miss you so.
Cars came and went–
so did Alyssa, Julia, and Andrea (a Creed fan);
Two of those three enjoyed plastic covered back seats.
Jim, Rueben, Rodger, Dana, and the Joes
threw up back there years before.
Plastic covered jokes,
sneaking smokes,
driving drunk.
We used to have fun.
I used to smile.

Balloons tied to tailpipes always pop.

People And Their Babies on Facebook

People and their babies on facebook.
Oooooos and awwwwwws,
seeking a stranger's approval.
Even when their baby is ugly.

People and their babies on facebook.
Have no shame and talk about their days–
"Baby ate green beans!"
Like we care.

People and their babies on facebook.
Posting photos for their girlfriends' approvals–
"Say cheese, little baby!"
Click "Like" and "Comment" with "So cute!"

People and their babies on facebook.
Thinking they've done something great by making a baby–
like no one's put a penis in a vagina before to make a baby!
B-O-R-I-N-G

People and their babies on facebook.
Thinking they've done something great
by sharing their babies faces on the facebook
Have we forgotten that babies are expensive, smelly, and somewhat bald?
LOL

Throwing Oranges In The Air

Oranges and apples.
Blondes and brunettes.
Cows and dogs.

The latter is not a guarantee-
the former not always means the latter;
and the latter never guarantees a ladder.

Double ts and double ds.
Big butts need larger chairs.
In the air like you just don't care.

Throwing oranges in the air like you just don't care.

Irish Brian Kelly: *Poet, Engineer, Landscaper, Lover*

Men Of The Highest Intellect

Seeking shelter from the literate and the articulate,
I hit the town.
Traded in a Bachelor's degree for a shotgun and a fishing pole.
I made life plans.
Parked myself at the Baseball Tap with the cowboys in Cherry Valley,
Illinois– not Texas.
Made some friends and learned their racist jokes.
Laughed out loud to not get shot, but white people aren't funny.
Wallowed myself with warm cans of beer, and the conversation was cheap.
My 'hell nos' became 'hail naws' after three hours.
'Come on, what do you think, man?' became "Wacchu talkin' bout' frand?!"

Progress on the plan had advanced.

Seeking shelter from the literate and the articulate,
I traded in the company of righteous friends for fishermen and hunters.
No need to be the teacher's pet or the teachers friend.
Entitlements and me, me, mes.
I traded in my degree for a new dialect in Cherry Valley–
Again– Illinois, not Texas.
Guns, boats, canoes, and fishing poles.
We spent the summer on the river pretending to catch fish we can't eat;
so we throw them back.
In the fall we dress up like John J. Rambo–parts 1, 2, and 3–
searching for a 13 point Monster Buck.

I Mash Potatoes On My Face, What You Do Today?

When we don't find dem–the Monster Bucks–
we still get fucked up at the Baseball Tap in Cherry Valley,
Illinois– not Texas.

"Remember dat one time Ol' Ron Dickinson bought a round for us last fall
and we laughed at his racist jokes-
even though they still weren't funny?!"
Yaz, I 'member dat.

Ol' Ronnie Dickinson caught me thinking 'bout my righteous frands
(those who are literate and articulate)
and by golly, Ol' Ronny D. called me out:
"Hey now smarty pants, why you thinkin' so hard?
I saw you in the field aiming at your face instead of deer.
That gun's made for huntin, boy, not for thinkin."

I'd forgotten who I was for a moment,
and where I was,
who I've been,
and the people I don't fit in with.

Here we are again. my righteous friends.
With books for readin' and backs made for stabbins'.
Let's kill some bucks,
catch fish,
but don't forget what those 'billies in Cherry Valley taught ya:
Throw 'em back.

Men of the highest intellect.

Teachers Taught

Teachers by the thousands fight, fight, fight!
Teachers by the thousands cry, cry, cry!
Teachers by the thousands fought.
There are three or four out of one-hundred and forty plus teachers,
that I've met, sat, and listened to,
with names worth remembering.
"That's not good math,"
teachers taught.

Upchuck

Reflections bounce off the ceiling paint;
Christmas lights in the month of May.
It's you,
throwing me up in the room.

Lint from the rug sits up by the dog;
take him for a walk just so that he feels the love.
It's you,
throwing me up in the room.

Bored and callous lovers hanging out in the yard;
married life in general- just give me a gun.
It's you,
throwing me up in the room.

Stop to smell the grass maybe pee on a tree;
all the careful mowers looking right back at me.
It's you,
throwing me up in the room.

Sit by the ducks, maybe throw them a rock;
the water's never blue here- it's always brown.
It's you,
throwing me up to the moon.

Irish Brian Kelly: *Poet, Engineer, Landscaper, Lover*

Light a candle
it feels like winter.

Fight the neighbor's noise,
it's time for dinner.

Looking out for Leonard's lover,
she's a winner;
trading books for lovers looks,
she's my December.

I could find a thousand ways so you'll remember
what it's like to draw a heart stitched to a letter.

All the calls on this machine are stuck on forward;
stupid thing it never works,
return to sender.

Drop a deuce now and that feels good;
all these careful, careful, careful thoughts of you.
We rhymed alot then and now it hurts,
let's drink Maalox til our eyes are blurred.

You fooled me, dear, with the winter;
it's you
–the darker side of you–
Throwing me up in the room.

Firecracker Empty

Firecracker
empties
song-dust
gently
on
my
pillow
tonight.

Firecracker
empties
flowers
folding
gently
on
my
pillow,
tonight.

Party People

Party people always go where the party goes.
Dare to join if invited; protect your soul.
Wear glasses, yawn, and be warned:
The more you drink, the more you'll know about so and so,
and so and so.
When you go, you'll never know–
now you're the talk of the town.
Party people always go where the party goes.
Find a hole and hide.
In your home or somewhere else.
Wait for cars stopping by.
Bright lights and white lies travel fast through the night.
Party people always go where the party goes.
Close those blinds wherever you hide and try.
Try blocking out rumors and lies.
The party always goes where the party must go with or without you.
You are never forgotten, they will shit your name.
Cocks and cunts always go where cocks and cunts must go to party.

GO GO GO, PARTY PEOPLE, GOAL!

I Mash Potatoes On My Face, What You Do Today?

Ha Ha Ha, LOLs and OMGs!

that foot filled this face page with patchouli
cantaloupes bounced around this brain
a double 'd' for you and me, but mainly for me

the piggy barks at midnight,
"Where are my milk and cookies?!"
Where art thou melks and cooky!?

I pithy the pool for a blanket made of wool instead because I can
Women watching dancing with the stars always ask,
"WHAT DOES THIS MEAN?"
CUANDO DOS NARANJES!? WHOLE QUE!

What do you mean?
Oink oink, bah bah, mooooooo
HAHAHA, LOLs and OMGs

Ditches and Holes

bitches and holes
don't make french toes
but the kitchen man can

witches and toast
can't make pot roast
in the butter stick pan– can you?

with the eggs in hands
if the chicken legs ran
man watt-choo gonna do?

ditches and hoes–not holes or toes
for a farmer's tan land
when he eats french toast

with a side of buttery bitches and holes.

Fisting The Air

the air is right
the end is near
filled up a few bags with grass
all those little mother f*ckers are growing back
the sky's gray
and no one's laughing
maybe a good day for cameron's warm songs
and pounding beers
and cursing names
and fisting air instead of faces

Again and again

I've filled up a few bags with grass
but all those little mother f*ckers are growing back
the air is always right
the end is always near

Lady, Do You Wanna Be My Baby?

B*tches be lickin'
(Ungh)
Doggies be trippin'
(Whuh?)
Butter on the toast and all the mother f*ckers wanna' eat it
but you won't
(Damn gurl watt choo drinkin?)

Lady,
(Yeah that's right I called you a "lady")
You gotta 'lots to learn
if you wanna' be my baby.

Hetero Dudes Named Todd Who Are Really Good At Sports Stuff

Hot water fails at your feet
into a frozen sheet;
you're that fucking cool

The pass from my hands
was hot and fast- but you still caught it;
you're that fucking cool

I couldn't do what she wanted me to
but you did and she liked it;
you're that fucking coo.

I love you Todd
you're everybody's friend;
you're that fucking cool
you're that fucking cool
you're that fucking cool
I'm not

Unlucky Men, Orange Women, and Ugly Children

My baby took me to the grocery store today.

It's Saturday, the worst day in America to be anywhere.

Many people gathered around the vegetables, breads, and fruits.

Some with children, some were bathed beforehand.

Maybe. Probably not.

It wasn't negativity that crept in, but something else.

(Minority call it reality.)

Bacteria was definitely in the air and landing on produce.

I saw it happening:

Finger tips to lemon skins and everything in-between.

Unlucky men, but mainly women with their ugly children.

Rules of the road need not apply.

Park to the side OR GET OUT OF THE WAY.

DON'T STOP THERE, c'mon.

Are you kidding me?!

There are other people behind you, Lady–

Jesus Christ, c'mon, it's not that hard.

 I LOVE THE MILK AND CHEESE AISLE, TOO! F*CK.

It's the best day in America to wander aimlessly like a cow in heat,

but don't look at me like that lady.

My girlfriend is here and she saw you.

She asked me if I saw the hot milf and I said, "What milf?"

Today my baby took me to the grocery store.

Unlucky men, orange women, and ugly children everywhere.

Lo And Behold, The Power Of The Milkbone

MOTHER FUCKERS BE TRIPPIN'
DOGS BE RIPPIN'
ASS ON MY PILLOW
TONIGHT

COME ON, DOGGIE!
WOOF WOOF!
LO AND BEHOLD, THE POWER OF THE MILKBONE
DO YOU WANNA
GO FOR A WALK?

HAHAHA, NO WAY, PUPPY!
IT'S TOO LATE
GO NIGH-NIGHT!
OK? OK!

MOTHER FUCKERS BE TRIPPIN'
DOGS BE RIPPIN'
ASS ON MY PILLOW
TONIGHT

Ronald Reagen Was A Very Good Man, Maybe

Ronald Reagen
was a good man,
maybe

Ronald Reagen
was a good actor,
maybe

Ronald Reagen was good at a lot of things
I think,
but I can't remember

One thing's for certain
with regards to Ronald Reagen,
he wasn't a very good president

If I were An Ironic Man, I'd Grow A Beard

If I were an ironic man,
I'd grow a beard

If I were an empty balloon,
I'd fill me with air

If I were a dead billionaire,
I'd pay the Chinese to make my iPhone, too

If I were a vagina,
I'd put my penis in a condom before making love to me because I can't afford to raise children in such a beautiful world that is dictated by social class, money, material possessions, and fucking assholes

Looks like I have to settle on growing a beard

LITTLE FISHY WANTS ME TO MAKE A WISHY!

OH, YOU WANT ME TO MAKE A WISHY, LITTLE FISHY?
DO YOU WANT TO CHOKE ON MY PENNY?
OH YOU DO, LITTLE FISHY? WHAT?!
WHAT YOU SAY TO ME?!

"Toss me your pennies and make me a fucking wish.
I'll make sure the other fishies don't take your pennies if you give them to me. Lol. Idiots!"

YOU WANT TO MAKE IRISH BRIAN DREAMS COME TRUE?!
AMERICAN DREAMS?!
MAKE A WISH COME TRUE?!
WHAT?!
YOU CAN'T, LITTLE FISHY!
YES, YOU CAN'T!

CHOKE ON IT LITTLE FISHY!
THERE IS MY PENNY,
YOU EAT IT!
I MAKE A WISHY, BUT LOOK AT YOU NOW LITTLE FISHY!
YOU CHOKE LITTLE FISHY, CHOKE!
OH NO!
LITTLE FISHY CHOKE ON IRISH BRIAN WISHY

Today Is Always A Good Day To Buy A Speedboat In America

Water waits for my arrival.
That speed boat I saw sitting in Bill Dixon's driveway is really nice.
Cherry Valley's residents have really nice boats.

Ol' Bill sells a hard sail,
"We're a long way from Dublin, Brian,
and the gangs and the street fights.
You would really look good in this boat–
making waves on the Kishwaukee.
The locals will be jealous,
or pissed drunk at the Baseball Tap–
especially when the water is high."

The people in Cherry Valley, Illinois are really nice;
if you look beyond many of their racist jokes
and brand new fishing boats.

Mr. Dixon bought a speed boat
but really wants a fishing boat
like his neighbor, Steve Coates.
They want to fish together.

I thought about this really hard,
and told Mr. Bill Dixon,
"You see, Jim, I've never been white enough to do these things white people
do in America; golf was never my thing and hunting appears to be the one
step many don't take , or can afford to, after playing with action figures and
video games;
but today could be the day to buy a speed boat!"

You bet cha, Bill!
Tell your neighbor, Steve, "it's time to go fishin!"

Today is always a good day to buy a speed boat in America!

God's Garbage Lives Here

See the filth festering from fake smiles–
the faces of peasants.

Poor people everywhere,
complacent and proud about it,
strangely.

Feel the pot holes,
taste the debris,
be religious.

Christian coffee awaits you after church on Saturday nights,
but you'll opt for an all-night bender, baby.

"It's worse than what we may have thought it used to be, Jojo–
God's garbage lives here."

You and me are value meals filled with french fries;
tossed out of passing cars by privileged hillbillies.

Look around:
litter for the learning
and nothing earned for working.

SUVs with vanity plates reads our minds at every stop light,
beware.

Carry a card that reads,
"Feed the squirrels and poison the peasants
but guard your thoughts–
for we are only minions amongst many.
Oink oink,
bah bah,
moo."

This is our birth town;
this is where we used to dream about getting out–
now we dream of dying everywhere else.

Rockford, Illinois
61103

The East Side Is A Wrench

"The east side is like a wrench when it comes to culture.
Culture is not strip malls and chain restaurants.
White people f*ck everything up."

So said Denver's Peter Lemonjello about his hometown,
ROKE FART,
ILL ANNOY.

Whiteys leave a stink when they sprawl
away from the city
and back to the farm.

Trees, gone.
Animals, lost.
Ecosystems destroyed by union deals, tax breaks,
and awful, poorly planned, urban engineering.

Yes, Mr. Lemonjello,
white people do f*ck up,
everything.

First Time Home Buyers Plan

Don't worry, you can afford it.
Buy a house you don't have enough money for.
Do it, do it for the man.

Don't worry about facts or math.
Who cares if you don't make enough, it's America!
Do it for the man!

Fill the homes with those that pay until banks refuse to help.
Work with the man on a federal funded, first time, home buyers plan.
Take his cash for a house you can't afford.

First time home buyers:
Save your money and avoid the plan;
or this will be your last.

Dr. Rob

For weeks on end we met.
Every other Wednesday at 9 or 10am.
Gently removing a manilla folder
with my name on it
from his bottom left desk drawer,
he'd ask, "So how are we doing this week?"

Rob was his name.
His uncle, a pitcher for the Tigers;
his wife, a psychiatrist for the city;
his daughter, married to a nice guy, but unemployed like everyone else
and foreclosing on their house;
in Carolina– north or south?
I did not verify.

Economic times we live in worry Rob.
He said to me one morning,
"Your generation is a write off.
I feel bad for all of you.
There are fewer reasons to work hard and nothing to show for it.
No insurance, retirement, a return on investments is nil."

He also told me of his love for horses,
black angus burgers, and cowboy boots.
Vacations with the wife, repeatedly to Nashville, frequented each session.

They met Vince Gill one night at a diner near the Ryman.
Rob liked country music.

Sometimes we'd talk about divorce, depression, anger, resentment,
forgiveness, and other reasons why I went to see him.
I doubt he really knew what I was thinking,
but it helped to listen to him.

Maybe not. I don't know.

Sitting there and smiling at his stories reminded me, IrishBrian,
how wonderful life is–and can be–in the company of Americans
who have lived it and want to share their stories.

I also realized how insane everyone is or will become.

Rob's stories were cheap and therapeutic.
He only charged $35 for each appointment,
and the remaining $115 to my insurance.

We met for over a year to consider my problems and talk about his life
until his wife got sick and passed away from cancer during our sessions.
I hope he's ok.

I learned how to listen to life from Dr. Rob,
the therapist.

Almighty Clooney Syndrome (ACS)

Dr. Doug Ross keeps getting grayer
and women are getting bigger;
but his women always get younger.
Trade in yesterday's model for a new one, a tighter one.
Wait for the switch to flip;
no more jokes, no more sex and the let the talks begin:

"George, can we talk?"
Yes, dear.

"Where do you see us in a year?"
France. The set of Ocean's Eleven Part V, I don't know– why?

"I'm getting older, George–and don't get mad, I know you told me in the very beginning about how you felt towards getting married again, babies, and raising a family. You've been very honest with me but I want a baby, a family, all the things a girl would want, I want with you."

What do you want me to say?

"Anything, George, anything- where is this going? I need to know."

Listen, sweetheart, I love you– but you know where I stand and you knew on day 1 how I felt about all that domestic huh bub shit. I have a career to sustain, my life's work. It will last longer than anything we are, or anything you want. You are asking me to provide a peasant's dream. I can not.

"No, George, I don't know where you stand! All of this peasantry is too confusing! Talk to me! What about what I want? Is that not important?"

What about what I know I don't want? Remember day 1? You didn't listen. You never do… Let me rephrase it for you, "No one listens to me." Case and point. It's time for you to go now. The women are waiting for me at the Villa.

Population control problems, help is here:
The Almighty George Clooney Syndrome.

Hillbillies In Bergner's Suits

Clock blockin,
thought blockin,
why yawl answerin' to hillbillies in Bergner's suits?

Don't tell me you gots to pay the bills, baby!
Those bills can wait–
Your ass gonna die at that desk answerin' to hillbillies in they Bergner's suits!

What I say?!
No bitch! I dint say, "fish filet"!
I said you gonna die doin nothin with your time if you think we here to answer to the white man and his cheap ass Bergner's suit!
What?!
Damn you dumb, gurl!

Before you know it,
all the dreams you had,
and words you wished you written–
are as good as dead.

Dumb ass, white mother f*ckin' hillbillies in Bergner's suits runnin they biz
don't give a shit-
isn't it about time you and you and you and you and you and you and you
did?

Clock blockin,
thought blockin,
why yawl answerin' to hillbillies in Bergner's suits?

Not Even The Wind Can Feel Me Spread So Thin

Nothing more, nothing less.
Spread so thin not even the wind can feel me.

HA HA!

Ready For The Next Unless This Is The 9th

Ready for the next
unless this is the 9th.
Oh well, if it is.

Say "so long" to the universe,
powerful and evil, true–
too big to be good.

Ready for the next
unless this is the 9th.
Oh well, if it is.

Horrible People Are Winning

Too comfy with losing,
horrible people are still winning.
Retributive justice may be in order,
but not from the law.

That is the only way to stop horrible people.

Poison sleep patterns
with bad math and property taxes.
Unlike Wall Street and banks for sale,
American dreams are fixed to fail.

Retribute the silent act,
poison the well with zeros and dollars,
real dollars made of paper, use them–
now throw the credit away,
it's money that doesn't exist to begin with.

Sit back, look, listen-
watch losers become heroes
and rebuild.

That is the only way to stop horrible people from winning again.

Lit A Match For My Lady Frand

Lit a match for my lady friend this mornin'.
I said, "Phew, wow, glad that's over."
She said, "Did you light a match?"
I said, "What you thank woman? Hail no. This ain't no campfire."
She was like, "Ugh. I have to go pee."
I just lit a match for my lady friend!

TONIGHT THE TRAPPER TREATS THE LADIES TO THE BUTTER BURGERS and THE BRUCE SPRINGSTEEN

TRAPPER SINGS THE SONGS
HE SINGS THE SONGS FROM THE BRUCE
FROM THE SONGS HE SINGS THE BRUCE TO THE SPRINGSTEEN
FROM THE SPRINGSTEEN TO THE SONGS
HE SINGS THE BOSS' SONGS FOR THE LADIES
FOR THE LADIES DO NOT KNOW BETTER
BUT THE BOSS KNOWS WHICH SONGS
THE TRAPPER WILL SING TONIGHT

TONIGHT HE SINGS THE SONGS TO THE LADIES
TO THE LADIES TRAPPER TREATS THEM WELL,
HE SINGS AWE KNIGHT:

"Strap your horny hands across my engine, ladies!"

HE TREATS THEM TO THE DOUBLE BUTTER BURGERS
WITH BACON
FROM THE BRUCE TO THE LADIES TO THE BUTTER BURGERS
WITH THE BACON
AND FOR THE BABIES THEY WILL MAKE TONIGHT

FROM THUNDER ROAD TO MILWAUKEE,
ALL THE LADIES CRY OUT TO TRAPPER TONIGHT:

"Lick my butter burger baby and take me down to Atlantic City!"

LADIES AND THE BRUCE AND TRAPPER
AND THE BUTTER BURGERS WITH THE BACON
DON'T FORGET THE CHEESE CURDS AND BBQ DIPPING SAUCE
DEW KNOT FOUR GHETTO EAT THEE CHEESE CURDS, LADIES!
YOMMIE!

DO IT FOR THE BABIES IN THE WISCONSIN TWO KNIGHT!
MAKE THE BABIES IN THE WISCONSIN TONIGHT!
TONIGHT! TONIGHT!
THE LADIES WILL FIGHT!
TONIGHT! TONIGHT!
THE LADIES WILL FIGHT FOR THE TRAPPER'S LOVE TWO KNIGHT
BUT THE BRUCE ALREADY EAT THE TRAPPER'S HEART OUT
TODAY AND YESTERDAY AND TOMORROW
HAHA LADIES, HOW YOU LIKE HIS VELVET RIMS NOW?
ALL OF TRAPPER'S TOMORROWS ARE BRUCEY'S YESTERDAYS!
EVERYBODY WANG CHUNG TWO KNIGHT!
LADIES LOVE TO WANG CHUNG FOR THE TRAPPER'S LOVE TWO
KNIGHT BUT THE TRAPPER WILL FEED YOU THE BUTTER
BURGERS WITH THE BACON AND SING TO YOU THE SWEET
SPRINGSTEENS, BABY! DO IT FOR THE TRAPPER AND THE BRUCE
SPRINGSTEEN!

I Mash Potatoes On My Face, What You Do Today?

WHAT IS YOUR FAVORITE INANIMATE OBJECT?

Celtic chairs.

I Knew Then What I Still Know Now

been depressed an entire life
half-dead as long as I can remember
failed kindergarten for a simple reason
that still holds true now more than ever
I don't like people gathering in herds

I knew then what I still know now

Follow the herd into the slaughterhouse
or standby and laugh at it all

I knew then what I still know now

Don't feel bad, no, don't be mad
I'll be laughing with you, all of you, in the end
Some of you are mother fuckers
and some of you are lambs
but some of you are god damned stars
burning brighter, burning faster than the rest

been depressed my entire life
as long as I can remember
failed kindergarten for a simple reason
that still holds true
now more than ever

GO GO GO, BONO, GOAL!!!!

Saturday Night Anthem Written During The Thursday Night Blues

I'm going to be so drunk by 7 a.m.

You will understand why Mars is red
You will know why Reagen hired Mr. Bush
and his evil frands

I know now and can't tell anyone
No, not until 7 a.m.
Not until her panties are around my head

Saturday night anthem,
Thursday night blues

How Easily People Forget

how easily people forget
why people punch people
how easily people pretend to be forgiven
after fucking another's woman and man
alcohol calming conscience
cocks and cunts be crying,
"I'm sorry! I drank too much!"
Easing all inabilities to be trusted
how easily people forget
why people punch people

Everyone Here Will Die Of Alcoholism— I Couldn't Care Less

stupid, drunk village

pissing lives away

automatic urinals

flushing lives away

evil serving evil

exiling lives away

everyone here will die of alcoholism

I couldn't care less

Irish Brian Kelly: *Poet, Engineer, Landscaper, Lover*

Are You Uncomfortable Yet?

Are you uncomfortable sitting Indian styled?
Ams spread out like a God-Damned Eagle, bald, on the edge of a couch?
Legs crossed at the ankles with hi-tops and rolled jeans.
Part-gelled and half-moussed hair, broken glasses and medicated zits.
I stared at Scott Norwood on the television while he missed that field goal
for the Buffalo Bills in the Super Bowl.
Everyone seemed shocked.
I felt nothing.

Earlier in the evening, my friends lit me on fire with a cigarette lighter.
Smoke rose from the bottom of my hoodie to the top of my neck.
I quickly realized what the smell of burning hair tasted like.
Rueben rolled me on the ground to put out the fire.
Everyone laughed.

Try forgetting your friends set you on fire
and you'll understand why the definition of "friends"
has been dead to me since.

Start a fire, burn my bridge, try to, but beware:
Bombs away.
A life-time of paybacks.
Are you uncomfortable yet?

Blowing Your Wings Off

got a fox
river on radar
l.a. to new york to tennessee
everywhere
the smoke monster trails
blowing wings off
it stops here
one more drink
cheers
here's to you
blowing your wings off
little bird

Dessert Never Came So Hard On My Face

spicy pasta

passed for panties

just as hot and soft

laced up at the hips

I licked my lips

and waited

and waited

and waited

it must've been a dream

dessert never came so hard on my face

I Mash Potatoes On My Face, What You Do Today?

Cow, Pig, Doggie, Bear

I don't care
I'll be voting for a cow, pig, doggie, and a bear

I don't care
A man can marry a goat if he wants to
A woman can marry a shoe, or two
It's all in our heads
don't tell me what I can and can not do
I will marry all of you if I want to
I will do it and eat this shoe, too, because

I don't care
I will never forgive you
and now I don't care
I don't care
I don't mean to rhyme or reason why
but I don't care.

I don't care
I'll be voting for a cow, pig, doggie, and a bear
Sharks, fishies, and red-tailed foxes, too
LOL

I don't care
I don't care
I don't care

Irish Brian Kelly: *Poet, Engineer, Landscaper, Lover*

Whiff, Whiff, Whiff – The Sound Of Peasants Thinking

drop the bat

catching fastballs in midflight

curve balls don't bend at the eyes

or break at the knees

throw that garbage back

whiff, whiff, whiff

the sound of peasants thinking

Single Mothers On Weekend Benders

fish kiss

pucker lip poses

internet photos

bedazzled cigarettes

feeding vegan purses

blind boys buying beer cans

filling desperate hands

bling jeans blinking

baby-making moves a shaking

practicing exemptions

single mothers on weekend benders

Irish Brian Kelly: *Poet, Engineer, Landscaper, Lover*

Spitballs And Empty Bic Pens

spitballs and empty bic pens

venom tucked away

a memory's reservoir awaits

hall of fame expatriates penciled in

those late eighties all-stars, it's their first time

remember that time you set me on fire

in the basement of the house on Melrose?

everyone sat and laughed but me

we watched Norwood kick and miss wide right

second stringers and bullpen reserves have to wait their turns

but their time will come

the lineup card on judgement day requires a barrel of water

and a bucket to piss in

there's not enough saliva to burn everyone back in the end

spitballs for bombs

empty bic pens for canons

Hi Brian,

I was wondering:

Should I be concerned about the glaciers? Is all life interconnected? I can't tell who is telling me the truth about things. Are things unfolding as they should?

Everything is unfolding as it should.
Entropy, chaos can not be stopped.
Embrace it.

The glaciers will melt, they are melting.
Do not worry.

There is nothing we can do to stop the universe from revealing what it will with or without our assistance.

The Middle Class Is In The Can

pretend prophets
proud abouts and past tense abused
i can't stand it
the middle class is in the can

No Time For Told You Sos When The Sun Goes

No time for Told you So when the sun goes. Surrounded by EL OH ELS and OH EM GEES, softly, I succumb to clock killers in pretty homes like a duck–or a dick–to cool, cool water before the first freeze. I smile and say "Hello!" to Lance and his wife while we rake leaves that have dropped on over to us from Bob and Patty's trees. Lance yells something neighborly back in my direction, but I point to my ear buds as to express that I have music on when I really don't. "Sorry, Lance! I can't hear. Got my Seger on." Lance says, "What?" I say, "Nevermind! EL OH EL!" The sun is quickly dropping behind Chad and Linda's trees. "Chit-chat's not going to make these leaves disappear any quicker, Lance," I think to myself. There's no time for talking while Bob and Patty's mother fucking trees are dropping leaves, man. I thought of all the nice things we could talk about, but I've done it before to enjoy the same results: All domestic-chore related conversations turns into neighborly cross-examinations of prosperity and wealth that comes with home ownership and renting. "Oh, Jerry, he must do well. Look at his lawn mower," says Linda to her husband, Ronnie. Blind judgements from mankind's finest American dreamers. Those who want more-more-more, but are proud enough to know less-less-less. Their fictional Maker comes to strip them of their earthly possessions. They ask the same questions: "How's work going?" and, "What is it that you do again?" and, "You're home a lot, do you work from home?" Never ask questions in return for two reasons: One, because I don't care about what others do for a living. Two, I was taught by elders that I respect that it's very rude to ask strangers questions for answers I have no business in knowing. Invasiveness is not fucking cool. That's their business, not mine. Shut the fuck up, Lance. Shut the fuck up, Bob. Shut the fuck up, Chad. Shut the fuck up, Patty. I often ponder unmerciful, honest ways to end conversations from the get-go. You want to know me that bad, earn it. Mother nature is having a gas. Bob and Patty laugh at us from behind their bay window. I'm keeping loose tabs on them elders and their trees–dropping leaves everywhere, here and there and there and here. I'll have written a few songs about Bob and Patty, and maybe Lance, too, come spring.

There will be no time for told you sos when the sun goes.

I Am #1, You Are #2

I am #1

You are #2

We are #3

They are #4

Them be #5

Those are #6

Everyone else is #7

Bow before the one before you,

and I will bow wow wow wow wow for no one because

I am #1

and you are #2

Irish Brian Kelly: *Poet, Engineer, Landscaper, Lover*

An Ever Growing List Of Names

An ever-growing list of names written in a notebook sits nearby. I'll share it one day, but not today. I'm going to add a few more pages of names to the ever-growing list of names written in the notebook that I'll share one day, but not today. Nope, not today. I'll pretend like I didn't hear what I heard again today. Maybe today I'll write some songs, draw some pictures, change around the ever-growing list of names with new names and face, and imagine up an end scene or two. A few, final scenarios for the ever-growing list of names written in a notebook that y'all will definitely read about one day.

Try To Save A City From Economic Despair- You're An Idiot

Try to save a city from economic despair–
you're an idiot.

Mommy always said,
"Oh Brian boy, everything you knows are math and science!
EAT YOUR CABBAGE, BOY, EAT ET, EAT ET."

You're all goddamned idiots!

HA HA HA, EL OH EL, HA HA HA, YAY, YOU$A!

My friend Andy is a jerk; his friend Reggie is a dummy; Reggie's friend Alyssa is a sales rep slut; Alyssa's friend Sean used to get naked with her in the I.T. closet on Tuesdays at noon; Sean's monster buck hunting friend and boss is Lord Derby; Lord Derby is Thomas Derby, CEO and LORD of all in the YOU$A™ at DerbyReynolds.com, THE WAL-MART OF ADVERTISING; Andy and Reggie and Alyssa and Sean all answer to their LORD and you $hould, too. HA HA HA, EL OH EL, HA HA HA, YAY, YOU$A! METAL PANTIES®

I Mash Potatoes On My Face, What You Do Today?

Jealous Artists Working Day Jobs Will Be Happy Next Year, There Are No More Ideas

there are no more ideas

next year's gonna be different

I say that every year

might use my birth name more, if it pays

pretty sure it doesn't

gonna start a quiet company

hook my hands up to an IV

become a videogamer by night

an audio engineer by day

psychoanalyze other peoples' creations for kicks

judge them

befriend scumbag ad firm owners

for real y'all

furr rio hue' awe

el oh el

oh el oh

jealous artists working day jobs will be

happy next year

maybe

i don't know

no ideas, guys, none

GO, GO, GO, BONO, GOALLLLLL!!!!!!

HEARTS SPLIT LIKE CHICKEN BREASTS

TWO PLANETS COLLIDE

HEARTS SPLIT LIKE CHICKEN BREASTS

ONE'S DRIFTING TOWARDS SPACE

THE OTHER FOR A TEXAN BROTHEL

HAHAHA, BABY, HAHAHA

70% WATER VERSUS 30% LAND VERSUS CHAOS

NOBODY WINS

ENTROPY

HAHAHA, BABY, HAHAHA

I Mash Potatoes On My Face, What You Do Today?

IKEA TOILET MANUAL

1. EAT WHAT GOOD FOR MOUTH*

2a. FORGET HAYBOUT BRAIN*

2b. HAND HEART*

2c. HAND STOMACH*

3. ADJOIN BODY TO TOILET*

4. LEAVE THE POOP(S)*

5. RELAX BABY*

6. WIPE BUTT* (PAPER NOT INCLUDED, BOUGHT SEPARATELY)*

7. PUSH LEVER NEAR RIGHT SHOULDER DOWN*

8a. SUPPLEMENT RIVER*

8b. FEED THE FISHIES WITH THE POOP(S)*

*REPEAT 4xs / DAY; OR 1x EVERY 6 HOURS, BABY

Irish Brian Kelly: *Poet, Engineer, Landscaper, Lover*

The Inspiring Story of Barkley and Winslow

Chapter 1
Mr. Winslow Thought I Was Gay from The Day I was Hired on Dec. 1st, 2000, Until That One Day At Work, During the Summer of 2001, That He Figured Out I Love Ladies lol

Hi, I'm Irish Brian Kelly. This is how I became me after I moved to the poor and corrupt northern IL region from Dublin, Ireland. These are key events in my life that I want to share with you in a book, and not on the internet. All names have been slightly changed to skew the absolutely awful truths about real mother fuckers with real names who affect the happiness of others with their shittiness.

I spent the first few months of my employment in the United States figuring out that I made a huge mistake to leave my life as a freelancing Irish artist to be a full-time, multi-media designer and artist for a regional ad firm. I put on the front that I was often mute and without opinions during critiques and team meetings. (I use the word "team" lightly, as I'm often the one who helps others to be left without a team to help me in return.)

A few years in America had been under my belt already by the year 2000. I was still figuring out the American workplace, and out of the work place. I discovered that people love to meet because they can't do. Americans appear to be ok with conducting an all-talk/no-do society, which alters greatly from the hard work theories and ethics that our grandfathers and great-great-great ancestors performed to help build this once-proud country into the capitalist fat pig that it now is. To the slaughterhouse and onwards into our mouths; so becomes all pigs.

Alas, meetings are necessary in order to keep the peasants doing and privileged douchebags talking. No matter the country it seems, but here in America I discovered that there are no differences between mayors and princes, kings and CEOs, laborers and peasants.

Mr. Winslow was my boss, a Creative Director – I use that term "creative" loosely. His boss was Barkley, and ad firm owner. Technically, Barkley ruled over both of us. Neither had managed to earn my Irish peasant's respect after a few months on the job.

I learned from listening and observing that both men hadn't earned their job titles or salaries in the traditional "work hard and better opportunities would open up" American way. Instead, each man came from very wealthy, privileged, American families who provided them every excuse and opportunity not to work up until college was over.

In other words: "*Here is your trust fund. You have no debts. Your education magically paid for itself. The money you will now need to run your own business, because you will never work for someone else the way poor people do, is yours.*"

This is a very common way for privileged white people in America to succeed; to bypass the efforts of working hard for one's success and opportunities. As the old, irish folktale goes: You are what you are born into, and I was born into a sack of potatoes.

Barkley, a few years into running his own ad firm, had met Mr. Winslow, a college senior, during a trip to his alma mater in Southern Illinois to give a

I Mash Potatoes On My Face, What You Do Today?

"*This is how I succeeded after graduating from here*" speech. Mr. Winslow approached Barkley after his speech to show him his little design portfolio. For American college graduates in the 1990s, that meant, "*Look at my pretty fonts!*", and "*Look at my imaginary CD cover! Hire me!*"

As fate would have it when one privileged asshole meets another, Barkley hired Mr. Winslow to be a "Creative Director" before he had ever worked one job throughout his entire young adult life.

(Acquiring the role of a "Creative Director" typically takes around 10 to 15 to 20 years of focused career work experience to even qualify for such a title– for most idiots that can survive the 'eat or be eaten' mentality of being a skilled laborer in the advertising and marketing industry. However, times are now different.

The children of baby boomers were now inheriting their parents and grandparents money, and could cut corners to success. The age of self-entitlements kicked in way before the advent of the internet and the 1990s, but with such technology, greediness and ineptitude was fast tracked for fortunate individuals. Which is partially why America has become a strangely unethical, spiritually corrupt, and economic wreck.

Ok, back to Mr. Winslow, Barkley and me; this is my Irish-American story.)

Within the first few months of working with these American baboons, I realized that they were the sort of privileged white assholes who would dump the dirty work on people like me at 4pm for a next morning rush deadline to stay up and produce all night, so that they could go home to their wives and family by 5pm to enjoy mashed potatoes, and return at 8am to review what was produced overnight by Irish slaves like myself; and then demand that I produce insane last minute revisions before heading to another brunch meeting to secure a five to six figure payment on the ideas presented– while never thanking, or feeding, those who stayed up all night to make it happen.

(We hard working, potato peelers keep notes on you gross, capitalist, fucking pigs.)

Things got weird with Mr. Winslow and Barkley. They eventually caught onto my stone-cold, Irish silence, and would forcefully try to engage me in neanderthal-like conversations about disgusting midwestern American women, sports ball, shitty beer, expensive 'white people drugs,' the terrible music that both of them loved, and all kinds of American shitty shit.

Worst of all was the the stuff their wives did to their homes, or what their kids said in the car, and other topics I had little to zero interests in communicating about with two people whose combined intellect was worth less than a bag of potatoes.

Then it happened one day: I finally understood why these goddamned idiots were always trying to lure me, Irish Brian Kelly, into conversations that I had intentionally shut them off from. I realized that Mr. Winslow, $parkles, and a few of my "teammates" thought I was gay. A homosexual Irish man? Yes. They thought I was a homosexual Irish man.

I discovered it with the help of a very sexy American sales rep that they hired a few weeks after me, Miranda. Miranda had been asked many times if she thought I was gay over drinks and extended lunch benders with my co-workers who didn't work in the creative department.

(If any of you think this is strange behavior, you've never worked in advertising and marketing in America. It's the most pathetic line of work next to prostitution; which is more honorable than working in advertising and marketing, because at least you know what you're in for up front.)

Little did those goddamned amateurs know, Miranda had the sales rep hots for me and was calling me on the inner-office lines, outside of work, and meeting me for after-work drinks and food. The first time she did such I was caught off guard. Everyone in the firm was gone for lunch, a meeting, something. Everyone but Miranda and I, separated by three business floors.

Calling me from her office one day, she asked, "What are you doing up there?"

Working. Why?

"You ever think about fucking me?"

Huh. I hadn't before that call, but was willing to play along.

Miranda proceeded to engage in phone sex, "Blah blah blah, heavy breathing, I'm cumming, oh my God, don't stop."

I was happy for her and her orgasm, but I couldn't do much for myself due to my work station being shared by four other people in an open-air studio. I thought nothing strange of it and chalked it up to another American Lady experience.

Miranda laughingly told me one night at the tavern that "the people at work think you're gay, Irish Brian."

I asked her why.

"Because you don't talk to them. They think you wear weird glasses, and listen to weird music."

Huh. What a strange, proud, judgmental country America is!

Miranda enjoyed every moment of the office entertainment that they had created for themselves behind my Irish back to figure me out– which wasn't much to figure out. I like my ladies the way I like my potatoes and bacon: Taste, smell, look good and be strong enough to kill a man's heart.

Our "teammates" had no idea about Miranda and I, and they didn't need to have an idea. It was our business. I had nothing to lose being the incredibly handsome, creatively-gifted single Irish immigrant. All she wanted to do was get off because her man was too busy hanging with the dudes, drankin' beers, and being an average American with a small penis. The kind of American guys that lock down pretty ladies with money, homes, cars, and boats.

You see, people, humans need two simple things to survive: Affection (pussy and cock) and Security (money and strength). Excuse my blunt words, but it's true.

I Mash Potatoes On My Face, What You Do Today?

If one person is lacking one of those things from their mate, they will find another person who will supplement that missing need. Miranda didn't need me for security, she needed affection. The easiest way to find it in America is from the single Europeans with the sexier character traits.

It happened again one day: I lured Mr. Winslow and the "team" into a conversation about where my girlfriend "Andrea" and I ate the night before. Little did they know, I was having fun with Miranda in their presence by mentioning the name of a woman who didn't exist.

Mr. Winslow bit my bait immediately and rushed over from behind his aluminum-walled desk: "*You have a girlfriend?! Wow, I could have sworn you were gay!*"

Hook, line, sinker. I smirked at the douchebag and asked, "*Really? That's crazy. I love women, Mr. Winslow Why do you think that? Should I be concerned about your excitement for my sexuality?*"

He replied, "*The glasses, your taste in music, you never talk to us, your clothes. I didn't know you had a girlfriend... None of us know anything about you so we figured you were gay!*" Everyone laughed, but this mother fucking American douchebag was serious.

Mr. Winslow was raised in a wealthy, conservative, American family from a small Southern Illinois town. His family owned a chain of fast food restaurants— Taco John's. He loved Motley Crue, and used to jokingly state that there weren't any Chili's Grill & Bar restaurants where he was from. That's why we had to eat at the Chili's as a team on "Friday Fundays."

True story.

Chapter 2
Mr. Winslow Asked Me If I, Irish Brian Kelly, Did Anything Artsy This Past Weekend, And So I Gave The Entire Shitty American Company Staff a Shitty American Story About William Corgan, Irish-American Tea Drinking, Music Man

Over the course of a few years of having to listen and answer to Mr. Winslow's insanity, I had accepted the cruel reality that I was an Irish peasant to him, and all I had to do was pretend to smile to get paid so that I could cover my bills.

"Do anything artsy this weekend?" he repeatedly asked me during Monday morning meetings. I should've replied just once, "Yeah, I did, you fucking dick," but I always smiled, never cursed.

Lying to him and the others during these anti-productive meetings became performance art. After all, lying is the foundation and core principal of working in advertising and marketing.

One Monday morning in particular, I jokingly told the roomful of dipshits – myself, account executives, ad firm owner, secretary, designers and programmers, our fearless Director, Winslow, a market researcher or two – that I drove into Chicago to assist Billy Corgan (of Smashing Pumpkin fame) with rebuilding his home recording studio, but ended up mowing his lawn and left Chicago early to come home and finish my lawn.

They asked, "Billy who?, and I lied more and more and more. They believed

I Mash Potatoes On My Face, What You Do Today?

me, but they were never impressed. I enjoyed it all because it allowed me to sit there protecting my Celtic muse while fueling any random thoughts that could satisfy Winslow's little art-slave-fag assumptions of me.

I never let these people into my world. They were the types of people who couldn't be trusted with my personal time and information, let alone my trust in return. These are people who never offered to help me peel potatoes in return. Never, not once, and that is how I judge the characters of those around me– work ethics and empathy.

This tactic could be considered psychologically off, but it's how I survive within an American environment. Figure out who can be trusted, and who can't. Where I come from, if you open your big fucking mouth the way Americans do without thinking, you better be ready for silence in return. The calm before the storm, or as American douchebag know-it-all call it, passive behavior. Yawn.

It's a tactic I've used since grade school in Belfast called "shit for shit."

Devalue my time by asking personal questions at school and work without me doing the same to you–or asking for it, thus breaching any privacy one deserves to protect–and I'll devalue your time and disrespect your personal space in return with nonsense, lies, and lyrics from songs you probably haven't heard.

In some cases, I recite lyrics from shitty Bono songs, because Americans eat that shit up.

Shit for shit.

Chapter 3
Mr. Winslow Taught Me That The Same Privileged, White, American Douchebags That Many Have To Be Surrounded By In High School End Up Surrounding Irish Brian and other Smart, Hard Working Immigrants, Often Controlling Us in the American Work Place

Some work experiences reveal greater opportunities, not this one; not in advertising and marketing, which is the lowest ladder to career climb. There's one way to go if you're not the owner of an American Ad Firm: Exit out, find a new career. A pretty easy goal to accomplish.

One little awful lesson I learned early on from Mr. Winslow was that all the privileged white douchebags and bullies I met in America's high school would end up affecting me in the work place, too.

Simply put: Privileged, white, self-entitled, American douchebags rule the world.

"*Let it go*" is a term I've heard dribble out of lesser minds n' mouths for years, but as an artist you never let go what makes you work harder than the privileged douchebags. Absorb it all and carefully recycle it.

You're welcome, kid: That'll be $30,000 for the life lesson. Paypal me some money at: irishbriankelly@gmail.com

Chapter 4
Mr. Winslow Loves Møtley Crüe

That motherf*cker Mr. Winslow used to play Motley Crue out loud as if it were an ok thing to do to get inspired.

Lest y'all not know, it's never ok to play "Girls, Girls, Girls" unless you're miserably stranded on a fishing boat in Wisconsin with a bunch of neanderthals – and even then it's not ok if you have options to play something else. We had no choice in Mr. Winslow's presence.

Everyone should have standards to live by. You get one shot to do this whole thing called life your way. There will be many people who will try to change and curve your standards of living, to accept some bad shit.

Mr. Winslow wanted us to enjoy Motley Crüe and "Friday Fundays" at Chilis Bar & Grill together, but I don't have time for shitty American standards.

I am Irish Brian Kelly. I don't listen to shitty American music. I mash fucking potatoes on my face.

Chapter 5
Bob Dylan and The Boom Box Day

Mr. Winslow's Boom Box Day was some sort of teamwork building exercise he came up with for us to share our musical interests; which was more like an experiment in *"learning how to hate your co-workers even more because they share shitty music, and don't want to listen to someone else's shitty music."*

Good times for all.

I heard Motley Crüe, Jewel, that 'Milkshake' song in late 2003. If I needed any more musical validations that I didn't fit into this American life, this was it. The Boom Box Day was an awesome team building experiment that I gave up on after my first attempt to participate.

Mr. Winslow asked me to tell the "team" what I was playing overhead. This happened after a decent two minutes had passed after initiating my first attempt to partake in boom box day. Strangely, no one knew it was the sound of Bob Dylan's voice on "Like A Rolling Stone," the first song from his 1965 masterpiece album, "Highway 61 Revisited."

(I mean, you need more than two fucking minutes to figure out it's Bob Dylan? Really? You need to ask me to tell everyone who is fucking singing "Like a Rolling Stone"? Are you fucking kidding me?! Yep. Amateurs.)

Deana, a co-worker in the creative department, said, "Is this the Beatles?"

I spun around in my chair, looked at everyone and did not answer. I couldn't believe the lack of cultural awareness I was surrounded by in that awful

I Mash Potatoes On My Face, What You Do Today?

American work environment, a creative department none the less. A place where no one knows Bob Dylan's voice but me, Irish Brian Kelly? Wow.

I stood up and pressed the stop button, ejected the CD, and sat down without saying a another word to anyone for the rest of the week, or probably a few months if I'm recalling my youthful ways to shut people out for being fucking ignorant in my presence.

The 'Milkshake ' butt song is the last thing I remember hearing on a boom box day.

Everyone who is born in America should know Dylan's voice by the time puberty hits; whether you enjoy him or not, doesn't matter. Myself being born in Dublin can remember the nasally tone of his voice coming out of me Mam and Paps' radio in the kitchen as a baby. America has not been the dream I heard stories of back home.

One's own cultural existence should be quizzed, rewarded, or socially punished based on knowing Mr. Zimmerman's name and voice. American parents should be stripped of voting and breeding rights if one should sadly fail such simple tests like, "Who wrote 'Like a Rolling Stone"? Fail and be rewarded with an "Amateur American" card.

That's how I'd run America.

Chapter 6
Barkley and September 11th, 2001

There were many other verbal nuggets/offenses that these two clowns, Winslow and Barkley, would spray in my presence.

One of the least charming, unsympathetic statements I've ever heard come out of another human being's mouth occurred during the morning of September 11th, 2001. Barkley wasn't aware of the World Trade Center attack, and questioned what was being reported on our department boom box overhead. Radio station, 89.5 NPR out of DeKalb.

Upon telling him what was up in the world that morning, he said with a laugh, "There goes the economy!", and ran out of the room down the stairs to bother someone else with his privileged douchieness.

I stood there thinking, "You insensitive rich white American prick, fuck you," and turned off the radio and went for a walk outside to the gas station to buy a donut and some clarity.

The culture-less American swine I was surrounded by for a paycheck, and then that awful news that became stitched into our existence that morning, has never left me— my adopted American-Irish existence.

Many insensitive words were spoken that day about the economy by Barkley and Mr. Winslow. I'll never forget it, nor care to expound.

Chapter 7
Barkley and Winslow Taught Me How To Reserve Curse Words Until A Later Date

Never once did I reply to early offenses and verbals attacks with "F*cking douchebag," or "Go f*ck yourself," because I was still young, nice, ethical and full of hope for the future, my career, and the American experience. How that all changes after you've stood by your principles to be laid off more than once by privileged douchebags.

There is no reason to be kind in the northern Illinois region where the wrong people get ahead while hard working people bend over on a daily basis. Kindness and hard work rarely rewards better opportunities. Those opportunities never come if you don't stand up and tell a few people where to go fuck themselves for wasting your time, name, and finances.

I established complete contempt for my American work place environment because of my leaders there, and what I had to sit through and deal with for a paycheck: Barkley and Mr. Winslow.

In order to deal with it, I put these awful people with their awful ideals and opinions into my own personal work at night away from work to create something better from their shit. The colors of contempt for privileged douchebags are always with me and are used on a regular basis to fuel creativity. Take this book for example.

Chapter 8
Take Pride in the Fact that Most of You are Weirdos

It's no secret now, but I do believe that most of you are not doing what you were put on this earth to do. You choose to use a sliver of the potential that is right there inside of your brain waiting for you to unlock and learn how to use "it"– the muse.

It's a precious thing that can evade as quickly as it welcomes you, but you have to recognize it first before you can do anything with it to unlock your potential. Sadly, as long as one person answers to other people who challenge the human existence, and prefer that you behave or morph into the type of person that they wish you to be, you are no one. Nothing. A shell of a person.

This is why most marriages fail. The woman wants the man to be this and that, wealthier and more emotional; the man wants the woman to be that and this; sluttier and more logical. Eventually, no one is happy and everyone gets to fuck themselves off. Marriage is a beast unto itself for most people because no one is fulfilling their own potential while trying to fulfill another.

Here's an example of a bad marriage: Remove all the songs but one from your iPod, and there ya have it – marriage.

Here's an example of a good marriage: Buy an iPod and have me dump about 20,000 songs from different genres and artists on it; then, play it loud and think of me when you're fucking your spouse and you're actually into it.

Listen to all those songs! That's a good marriage.

I Mash Potatoes On My Face, What You Do Today?

I truly feel sorry for most of you because you choose to remain proud, safe and unknowing in your own existence, choosing to judge those who are different than you, and summing others up as being "weird" or "strange," when in fact it is you–with a majority of others like you who are the real weirdos–that inspire the minority weirdos like myself to do whatever we wish to. Take pride in that admission if you must, or go fuck yourself.

The idea of Irish Brian Kelly was loosely created on May 14th, 2004, by Mr. Winslow and Barkley when they fired me from the last awful American job I've ever had. They claimed that the American economy was causing them to cut jobs.

Me being the first choice to go because I was an immigrant, but to cover their legal grounds, they said it was because I was single and without a family to worry about. Thanks.

Privileged douchebags always have the same excuses to protect their wealth and legal interests. Mr. Winslow wasn't even man enough to sit in the room for the layoff. He coincidently left work early on that late Friday morning to go home for a half day to be with his precious family.

I packed up my stuff, didn't say a word or goodbye to anyone in the firm (who had no idea I'd just been laid off), and laughed at the fortunate opportunity I had been given with summer approaching on the ride home to my apartment. It was the best day of my life: May 14th, 2004.

Irish Brian Kelly was born that afternoon. Whoever I was before that day, with another's poor birth name on a pathetic, poor, dead-end career path, was killed off– and it felt great.

Chapter 9
Unemployment Is Awesome and It Separates American Amateurs From Irish Assholes

Let me tell you this: Unemployment benefits in America are fucking awesome if you are single, no children, no girlfriend or others to nag you about what you're going to do next in life. ESPECIALLY if you meet all of the credentials I listed above and live in northern Illinois – one of the worst regions in America to find a job and keep it.

Unemployment allowed me to reinvent my own existence; to throw away every wasted day having learned nothing good by working for privileged American morons.

It didn't hurt my self-esteem, either. As I saw it, I already paid for my own unemployment by being taxed more for working hard as a single Irish man in a country that uses my tax money to help others work less; to help many of those irresponsible single mothers raise their children, because someone forgot to wear a rubber. All that poor shit we do to help others–and there I was, already poor and overworked, overtaxed, living from paycheck to paycheck and not making enough to pay my student loans after a car payment and health insurance–and now fired and out of work because being single to Barkley and Winslow meant I was expendable. Thankfully, that I was!

Unemployment for me, based on my poor financial situation (which I can clearly admit two decades later, was created by the student loans I had to take out to earn my college degree in a timely manner, of which I still had to hold down a few jobs to get through those semesters alive–to eventually realize that education is worthless in America without decent jobs to pay those loans back), was amazing and creatively fertile because of the fortunate amount of already-taxed ambition I had to spend on myself for once.

I finally found the American Dream: Unemployment benefits!

I didn't need a bed, couch, TV, or all that material shit. That's what separates amateurs from assholes, and Americans from Irishmen.

I lived without an active phone line for 15 months once I was laid off. I never owned a cell phone until 2007. Communication with the outside world was easy– I didn't need it. I had no dreams or hope for the future, and that was ok with me.

I simply wanted peace and quiet, music and pencils, ink, paper and a guitar. My family and friends were always 2 miles away in Belvidere, an ocean sail away in Dublin, and we knew how to find each other. Letters, mailmen, and pigeons sufficed. I was more than OK. I was ecstatic to be alive, handsome, talented, poor, happy, and healthy.

Everyone was like, "Don't you want a girlfriend or a job?"

Uh, no, do I need it?

"Don't you want gas in your car?"

Uh, no, do I need it?

"Don't you want to save a little money to buy a house?"

Uh, no, do I need it?

"Don't you want to have your own family one day?"

Uh, no, do I need it?

Life was good, it was simple.

I wanted absolutely nothing that everyone close to me felt I needed– to be happy according to their definitions of happiness. You see, it's all those things that I was questioned about wanting that I believe cause people to be so fucking miserable. And I still believe such. America is a beautiful country that is filled with fake, miserable people who forget that immigrants like myself made this country great, while privileged, caucasian, capitalist douchebags and proud, elitist, illiterate hillbillies ruined it.

(Tell me to start thinking positive, and I'll tell you where to go fuck yourself.)

I had everything with unemployment: Ideas and a parked car, a futon in the sunroom that I never unfolded from the couch position, a 13" antenna TV, and a bean bag. That's all I needed.

One of my best American friends and his wife were so disturbed by the fact that I had no bed in my apartment when they passed through to see the place that they hunted down an unused bed from his grandmother to drop off in the empty bedroom that I never used. The floor and a throw pillow sufficed.

I preferred sleeping on the carpet in the living room. It was better for my back, but mainly because I didn't care where I slept as long as the door was locked and people who tried to influence how I should be living my life stayed the fuck out of my space. Fucking amateurs sleep in beds, truth. Irish soldiers sleep on hard wood, carpeted floors.

I slept in that single bed a few times– with sexy ladies who politely complained (after they got off) that it was a single bed for children or old people. Let me show you the options to help you decide whether or not you want to sleep here, Lady Luxury: Over here we have the floor with a nice carpet, and over there in the corner is a nice bean bag, but I prefer you don't sleep there because I sit there to eat and listen to music; and lastly, over there is the door to the steps that lead you out the door to your car which will take you home to your apartment. Here, let me walk you out.

"Do you want to come over to my place?" they would often ask once realizing how honest I was when I warned them how I live, and how little money I had.

"Hmm, no thanks, my car is out of gas and I'll have no way home if I want to leave early." Real life, Ladies.

Life was that good and simple. I had affectionate options with quick exits that didn't require work, money, or gas to be happy because of my good looks, honesty, talent, poverty, and unemployment.

Chapter 10

Life is Awesome with Less and if You're Fortunate Enough to be Handsome, Creative and Poor, Ladies Will Still Love You and Leave You Alone to Create because You Can't Afford a Couch or a Bed For Them to Occupy Time and Space In

I slept on the floor, read, sketched, composed songs and illustrations from ideas, ate bagels, pasta and the basics, rode my bike whenever, answered to no one. With the unemployment checks I collected until mid 2005, I paid rent, my car payment, insurance, and had enough for a little food and saved the rest. I didn't have enough money for serious expensive shit like health insurance or a girlfriend until late 2005 or 2006, and honestly, I didn't want or need either one. I was young, handsome, poor and healthy!

I loved telling women who had interests in me that I couldn't afford to date American women, nor get involved with anyone who wanted to see where I slept because I didn't have a bed.

I had plenty of lady "friends" who'd come and go. They never had a problem with how I lived and admired the idea that I believed in 'less is more,' but I knew what they needed in the long run. Each lady made it well known during minute 2 of any conversation that I was not type of guy who was ever going to be able to afford material shit and children. They loved my accent, which can be a problem in America, because many nice ladies aren't used to honesty and accents.

Am I proud of this behavior? Sure, I was single and honest. Most American women are used to being lied to by American pigs. Every woman who fell in love with me, without me reciprocating that behavior or emotional need, will tell you that I always put honesty on the table. Whether you like what I have to say or not, I couldn't afford to care because I was poor and Irish!

What I did learn soon enough, once the accent wore off, was that women hate honesty deep down, even though they desire it for surface-level companionship. It's almost easier to lie to American women so that you can be the asshole that they need you to be. So that they can move on to the next American douchebag-guy that they can test out for marital and fatherly qualities. Someone else who lies the best that they can divorce from one day.

If there's one thing I've learned how to do well, it's to always tell American women the truth and American men a pile of shit so that I have some sort of balance in my Irish Brian universe.

Chapter 11
When you got nothing to lose, you got no fucks to give and you Get to Enjoy Phone Sex With Horny Unsatisfied American Women

Unemployment for me was the happiest time of my life. I got to be alone when I wanted to, all the time. No stress, no call me laters, just perfect.

I had it made at the bottom of America's dream: Handsome, poor, talented, desired, smart as fuck with an equal amount of not giving a fuck anymore, and honest. Always handing people a bagful of shit honesty that they deserved whether they liked it or not. I had nothing else to lose but a 13" TV, not even a fuck to give. Not even a fresh bag of potatoes!

I sold most of my life's possessions during the summer of 2004. Half of my music collection (which has always been the drug of choice) on ebay.com which I had to do at my Uncle Liam's house on their 56k modem internets which was a game. Uncle Liam made Aunt Mammy pick me up to do the internets. No gas, no need to drive a car.

Sold my portable phone, which I only used in my apartment from 1999 til June of 2004 to have phone sex with Miranda from that terrible American work place I had been fired from. American married women love phone sex with single Irishmen. That's about all I learned from working with Barkley and Mr. Winslow.

Miranda used to call me to get off when her man was out doing fishing and monster buck hunting, or watching the sports ball games with his wolf pack frands. I'd tell you more, but it's phone sex–it's pathetic.

I Mash Potatoes On My Face, What You Do Today?

I saved up enough money from unemployment to buy my own Chinese manufactured Apple Macintosh G5 computer, assembled in California, by early 2005. I could be "marketable" and employable one day in the modern American world again, but mainly to fuck with privileged white people on the internet. I dreamt of being the troll that Americans forced me and other unemployed peasants to be.

I used my Chinese manufactured Apple Computer to apply for asshat American jobs that I knew I'd never acquire employment with by being honest on the applications versus lying– which is what more than half of working Americans do to get a job.

Lie, oversell your pathetic, proud existence. The American way. I chose the Irishman way: Drunk, blunt, an immigrant's honesty.

Chapter 12
The Dept. of Labor Instructed Me To Buy a Phone to Help Myself Find a Job But I Said No For 15 Months

I enjoyed every minute of those unemployment checks while coming up with even more creative and brutal honest tactics to keep northern Illinois area retail businesses from employing me at $7 an hour to prove to the Department of Labor that I was incredibly unemployable from the summer of 2004 until the end of 2005.

I applied, tried and tried, but apparently having a brain is not required in America. Myself and many have proved that it can hold a decent person back from having a job in poor regions like Rockford, IL, where rewarding self-entitled, proud amateurs with jobs is the more likely outcome.

The amount of times I heard, "Have you looked in Chicago?", and "You're over qualified, have you looked in Chicago?, and "You're over qualified for us, but have you looked in Chicago?" was a game that I learned to enjoy every minute of. Rockford business leaders wanted hard working people to leave the city and state. I couldn't even get a $7/hr. job, and that was ok to me. I loved unemployment!

I'd check my AOL account once or twice a week at my Aunt Mammy and Uncle Liam's house to see if anyone replied, and sometimes there would be an interview request along with a "Can we call you? What's your number? You didn't provide it on your application." Mostly rejections, some via email, many mailed.

Considering I don't do phones and I don't talk to people on them (waste of

I Mash Potatoes On My Face, What You Do Today?

fucking time), I always complied with such email requests to call me with a response like: "No phone calls, the baby is always sleeping. Please email or hand mail me a time, date, and place for us to meet in the near future. Insure that it is two business weeks, or 10 days, in advance of this correspondence. I'll be there with an expensive Mickey Mouse tie on that I bought a few years ago when I had a job and took my week off to visit Florida, unless you advise me not to wear the tie ahead of time. Thank you for the opportunity."

These sorts of simple submissions and email replies marked and guaranteed me for not earning the job opportunity. As designed. I loved proving that there was no work for a creative professional like myself to keep the unemployment benefits and paychecks rolling in.

Anytime I had to meet my work counselor at the 11th Street location in Rockford of Illinois to prove I was an able American that was willing to work, she would ask me to try this or that to find a job, and make me sit in their shitty Windows PC study room to use the State of IL's internets database to apply at local business that might utilize my skills, education, and experience. Ad firms, of which I warned her would never hire me, she'd have me apply to to satisfy her ego.

Not one replied to me, or her. She didn't understand real life or the job market, and more-so when I would laugh and say, "Silly American! You don't understand your own country!" She did not like that Irish Brian knew what was up with capitalist pigs. I figured that I had earned my unemployment benefits by paying for them already.

I'd do an hour of pretending to care, apply from their shitty Windows PC, and then interrupt my work counselor during her next unemployed client-appointment to provide her a list of companies that I sent resume copies to with phone #s for her to call for me in a week as a follow-up, since I had no phone. Ahahahha, God dammit, unemployment was awesome!

The Dept. of Labor counselor kept instructing me to buy a phone with one of my benefit checks, and reactivate my line, or to get in on some shady cell phone deal, but I stood my ground for almost 15 months, claiming I couldn't afford a phone, a phone line, and had no use for cell phones– which is still true. I finally gave in to a landline in October of 2006. I figured, let's have fun with an answering machine.

The Department of Labor counselor figured out how to get ahold of me eventually. I had enough side work at this point thanks to the fine folks at DesignWerks who took me under their wings and allowed me to use their office Macs and internets to survive, to be Irish Brian Kelly!

FUCK, I miss unemployment.

I was the happiest I had ever been in my entire life. One important thing to know is that I started working in December of 1988 after turning 14 with a work permit. I was fresh off the boat and filled with American Dreams! I had earned my unemployment benefits with years of hard, low-paying work.

I still consider unemployment as my first paid-for vacation that I earned the right to enjoy like others have. I had never taken a vacation or sick day while being an employed American, ever, but even worse, out of all the jobs I had in that amount of time, 16 year worth, only two offered paid vacation time: 5 paid days. Yeah. Keep the change, assholes.

I Mash Potatoes On My Face, What You Do Today?

I worked very hard up until that magical date, May 14th, 2004, to earn nothing, save nothing, broker than ever, in debt with student loans and then finally I got a break to enjoy life. The American Dream realized.

Unemployment was the most amazing summer vacation I've had in my entire life.

Best part about unemployment is that the employer who fires you, most often without just-cause, and in my case it was blamed on the economy, pays for it. Ahahahahhahaha! Choke on a bag of dicks ya homophobic douchebags, Barkley and Winslow.

I had the last word as I see it. A year and a half vacation that I'd already paid for over the course of 16 taxed years to end up in my late twenties with nothing but an amazing bean bag, a college degree, and a parked car with no gas in it. I still had more than most, and ten years later, same car, same problems, no fucks given:

Shit for shit, unemployment was a well-earned, return on investment.

Chapter 13
Having a Phone Ruined My Life, Earned Me Good Work, and Cut off my Unemployment- Happy Days Gone Again

Being unemployed was a happy, healthy time for me from the summer of 2004 until the winter of 2005, the birth of Irish Brian Kelly went down.

I lost 22 pounds, and I felt great. Women loved me and could never get a hold of me. Sometimes they would show up unannounced at 8pm, 11pm, 1am, 2:10am, 4am, 11am, 1pm, etc.– all in shifts. Life was perfect without a phone, and each lady knew from the get-go that I was untrappable.

Sometimes one woman would show up and meet another, I'd always make them feel at home, feed them chips and water. Some became friends. Some wanted a tryst. Others disappeared, and came back a stalking me whenever drunk.

Being around me was a gift, an Irish gigolo gift.

They loved my personal, poor minimalism, handsome appearance, sense of humor, clean floor, Adidas tear-away sweat pants, boxes of Irish Spring soaps, comfortable bean bag, warm electricity, courteous disposition, and faucet water; but mainly, let's face the facts, they all wanted my horse cock and a chance to trap my DNA with a ring.

For a man that couldn't afford to leave his own apartment, I was a lucky

I Mash Potatoes On My Face, What You Do Today?

man. You see, rumors fly and women are the worst with them, especially when they are drinking, playing bingo, watching soap operas, or having their hairs done. I was a wanted horse, but inquiring riders rarely passed my cultural awareness tests: If you listened to Incubus, Master P, and Aerosmith, sorry– there's the door. Bye, bye.

American ladies could've cared less about my financial situation once they realized they were in the presence of a European thoroughbred. I repeatedly made healthy, honest points to bring up my poor finances and debts every chance I got to keep myself from ending up in the position of buying dinner or putting gas in the car in exchange for physical affection and emotional comfort.

Some of these ladies bought me new clothes, winter coats, dined me, and all I had to do was let them play with the horsey every now and then. The joy they received from tearing open a gold-foiled Magnum XL wrapper sent them through the moon with anticipation!

Being single and unemployed was the happiest I had ever been in America. I had zero responsibilities, and enjoyed the fact that I was not responsible for anyone else's happiness but mine; unless it was paid for in food and clothes. Fuck yeah, America. Dreams come true!

I kept this all up until I had to get a landline phone in late Oct. of 2005 because TDS Metrocom said I needed one in order to give me the internets access in my apartment, which was done with a 100 foot long ethernet cable running through the apartment on the floor to provide me DSL, not 56k – the cable didn't wrap around corners or under the floor, it literally ran through the apartment in a straight line through multiple rooms.

Having a DSL line and phone line ruined my decor and minimalist approach to living. There was no way to hide the fact that my life was now ruined. I was connected to the world, and it was visible on my floors in every room.

A few work opportunities came up because of the landline and 56k installation; and then a thief of a lady I was incredibly fooled by kept showing up, because she could get ahold of me on the phone and the internets.

In the blink of an eye – I lost it all thanks to technology. My happiness went poof. Everything about what made me a happy person was gone because of the fucking phone and internet.

Misery settled in again.

I was making the monies with my birth name–not my adopted Irish Brian Kelly gigolo name–and unemployment got cut off. I was using my car more than once every two weeks; if it had gas in it. Even worse, I was buying dinner for one particular American, rich hillbilly lady that fooled me.

All of my happy days came to an end when I got a phone line and internets installed. It's a decision that I have regretted since, and will take to the grave with me.

Chapter 14
My Life as Irish Brian Kelly Strengthened as my Personal Happiness Disappeared Forever When I Bought a Cell Phone and a House in 2007

I can honestly say that whatever hope I had for rediscovering the happiness I had while being unemployed was destroyed and buried when I got a landline phone, and then drowned forever in misery with a cell phone and real estate purchase.

My first Chinese made cell phone was acquired in January 2007, and my first American assembled house was bought in March of 2007. I regret each decision and take fault. Clearly my head won over my heart. Not. All of it happened despite knowing that I wanted neither of those evil, American, financial objects in my life. I was forced–and incredibly fooled–into both material objects by a very bad person – an evil American lady.

I own these bad decisions, and I had a choice. I argued the importance of each material possession, but you people will never understand the amount of evil I was up against. I had no energy left over to fight such pedestrian, elitist hillbilly, white people lady problems while I was trying to work for myself.

The least of my concerns was a relationship that demanded more energy than my self-employment, and so I caved in many times to conserve time and energy for what mattered most to me: My work. The work of Irish Brian, not wasting time and energy on the material goals that define many evil, lazy people in America– not just ladies.

The phone acquisition: The evil lady claimed that she needed to find me when she wanted to, and that it was bad for me to be self-employed without a cell phone because people needed to get ahold of me. Coming from a person who didn't work for herself, or at all, I bit my tongue often. I was in hell, but couldn't see through her lies yet.

The home acquisition: The evil lady claimed that renting an apartment was terrible and owning my own home would be better for our upcoming marriage and my work.

The errors of hard working men often take root in their bad choices and poor character assesments of women. Evil ladies often come pre-packaged to fool and rob one of everything. This one did.

I still believe that owning a cell phone and a home is a waste of time, energy, and money; and the recession definitely backs up my beliefs on reasons to rent versus owning in poor American regions like northern IL. Particularly, Rockford, IL.

I was now in hell full-time. Completely removed from the happiness I had found on my own while unemployed, single, and desired by good ladies. I clearly fucked up. Those were some nice ladies. I was now claimed and damaged by an evil lady. I owned a real bed that the evil woman bought for my birthday so that she could sleep in my apartment instead of on the floor where nice ladies once napped with me.

I still own my faults. I could have tried harder to remain unemployed and happy, but I didn't. My American Dream now dead.

Chapter 15
Answering Machines Rule–
If You're not Home, You're not Available

If you work from home and you're not home, you're not available, leave a message. Nothing in business is that important that you drop everything when you aren't at work to return to work, to help some schmuck make another million while he boozes it up behind his wife's back with a few whores down in Mexico.

Medical and law enforcement people are the only people I can think of that are paid to drop everything, get to work. Help someone. Everyone else, fuck off– I'm not a doctor, and I'm not available if I didn't answer the phone.

With the cell phone and my answering machine being sabotaged by the evil lady who had me fooled into thinking that owning more material stuff was good for relationships, life and work became unmanageable despite being busier than ever.

I couldn't afford to hire a secretary, let alone ask a friend for help. (How does anyone help an Irish genius? You can't.) My newly married wife could not be trusted to handle a single dollar bill, let alone learn how to help me run my business. I gave her two tasks, and she failed at both which caused clients to contact me, asking, "I thought you said that was being dropped off yesterday?"

Not even the responsibilities of easy delivery drop-offs on project materials, documents, could be counted on. She was not right for me. In fact, she was a lazy, self-entitled American. I wasn't able to clearly see this fact until I removed myself from her evil presence.

I had no idea when money was coming in for work finished, and where the money was going. The more money one makes, the more problems one has to manage it, the more people and creditors one owes. Evil multiplies itself when money is present.

I paid off my car, and that was cool– I guess. It always had gas in it now, but I never drove it for pleasure, only for meetings– and a lot of meetings. Remember what I said in Chapter 1: People in America love to meet, not work. Here I was now, handling the meetings with lazy American fucks, and then working all night like the peasant I was born to be.

Another problem with being too busy is that there is no time to live, to be happy, and there is little time to find help for the work to be produced. There is no one I trust to help me with the work. Work I can do much more efficiently with less interruptions between the hours of 8pm and 4am. The business world functions between 8am and 5pm.

I'd often waste most of those hours talking on the phone, having meetings, letting someone else tell me what to do after signing my contract estimate and paperwork. These are people you meet with who enjoy long lunches and early exits from work, to meet again for pre-dinner ideas. The game of it all was depressing and anti-productive to me, a goddamn horse, Irish Brian Kelly.

Some of the shittiest people I've ever met have everything and do nothing but meet. Some of the most beautiful, kind people I've met have nothing and work two to three jobs, some four. So, go fuck your American Dream– it's dead based on what I've experienced face to face right here in the Rockford, Illinois region.

Add a cell phone into the mix and everyone needed me ASAP to do this, do that, can you meet now, can you meet tomorrow morning, can you get this done overnight, can you can you can you. It got worse with texting.

The only way I could deal with it all was with turning the phone off so that I could work, focus, do, and talk less.

Eventually, a few businesses didn't pay me for the amount of work I was handling because they figured out how to evade me and drag payments out longer when their bills were due months earlier. They caught onto my kind, overworked, short for time-to-talk-attitude, and abused it until I had to become the asshole for all good intents to remind them to pay their fucking bills.

To this day, many still owe me– including Barkley. Mr. Winslow doesn't owe me anything. If anything, I owe him a thank you for the vitriol and creative fuel he provided long ago.

I failed to learn 'the power of no' early on, and paid dearly for it while not charging enough to hire someone trustworthy and apt enough to assist. Add a large element of bad timing combined with an evil lady and being self-employed in America at the on-set of the national recession, and I knew my birth name was done for by 2008.

Irish Brian Kelly was about to make some fucking enemies with nothing left to lose.

Chapter 16
An Asshole Is Conceived

During the late afternoon of May 14th, 2004, Mr. Winslow took the courtesy to call me on my portable home phone, which would soon be deactivated by the end of May 2004, so that I could make unemployment opportunities last longer (see previous chapters). I had already figured out how awesome life was going to be within a few hours of being laid off.

Mr. Winslow wished me good luck and told me that the decision was a hard one, that I would be better off not working for the company and it came down to me being the single guy on a team with others who had families. I'll never forget the moment he called, because it was the first time I decided to be an asshole to him– the one time in years he tried to be kind to me.

I had already enjoyed a few beers and a pair of incredible orgasms with a lovely kind lady named Linda barely 3-4 hours after being laid off. It was a late, sunny, Friday afternoon piercing through my apartment living room windows. We were laying down on the floor listening to Teenage Fanclub's "Songs From Northern Britain," buck naked, laughing at Mr. Winslow on the other end of the line while Linda, who lived two apartment buildings away from me, tried to get me to laugh more at him on the phone while tickling my Celtic horse cock and balls with her tongue.

All I was thinking was: UNEMPLOYMENT IS GOING TO BE AWESOME.

Refusing his sympathy and good luck while getting my horse cock stroked and tickled, I reminded him briefly of many of his disrespectful ways: "You've disrespected me every day for the last three to four years. Thank you for calling me to wish me luck, but more importantly, I can finally tell you to go fuck yourself. You are a privileged, little, white boy, and I will insure that you and all little, privileged, white boys in America never forget my name from this day on until I die: Irish Brian Kelly– Poet, Engineer, Landscaper, and Lover!"

He said, "What the… I–"

"You heard me, Winslow. I should have told you sooner how to go fuck yourself for being an American doouche to me all those years. Here's one easy way to understand me now: Take a big, brown, rock-hard potato and mash it on your face, bubba. That's right. Mash that potato on your face, Winslow!"

Linda laughed. I was so into this moment, finally telling him what I thought of him and his shitty ways, how he treated me, that I forgot my horse cock was being tickled by her tongue on the living room floor of my apartment. Mr. Winslow was stunned, said he didn't know I felt this way about him with a chuckle. Everything with that fucking guy was with a douchey chuckle, like he was happy to finally set me off like an American asshole I had dreamt of being one day. That one day arrived.

"Seriously, man. Take a fucking potato and mash it on your face." I said it again with more force before hanging up, And that was that, click. Linda was turned on by this moment, as anyone should have been, and continued to treat me like the poor, mighty, newly unemployed Irish horsey that I became that day.

Irish Brian Kelly was fully conceived on May 14th, 2004.

Chapter 17

Epilogue:
Barkley and Mr. Winslow Mash Potatoes On Their Faces, LOL

Mr. Winslow proved his true douchieness by late 2004 by taking half of Barkley's client accounts to start his own business– that's the way it works in advertising.

(It's a douchey industry overall. Become the douchebag or get out when you can. Mr. Winslow chose to be a bigger douchebag. Most ad firm owners are called $cumbags. They are an advanced douchebag, basically. Winslow became a $cumbag, advanced douchebag. Lol.)

One of his sexy sales reps–Miranda, who I believe I mentioned a few times in this Irish folk hero story–who used to enjoy phone sex sessions with m eventually married her high school, American sweetheart. She found others to have phone sex with because I cut off my phone line by the end of May 2004. I would assume. I don't know. Phone sex is pathetic.

Miranda missed me being around the office. She would stop by my apartment to tease me with the possibility of naked lunch nooners, but she wasn't lady enough for Irish Brian. She couldn't stand the fact that I cut off my phone line after getting laid off. She missed the phone sex and wanted to ride the horsey, but was afraid to because of being married. I get it, whatever. She didn't like the fact that I lived so minimally, either. The absence of a real bed really turned her off.

Miranda would take a nap on my futon and beg me to tell her what she wanted me to do to her while she fingered herself off. As if we were still on the phone, but not. I like weirdos, but what a weirdo. Whatever, come away.

She would make herself a bagel from my little kitchen to actually prove to herself that she came over to my apartment to have an Irish lunch, and not to cheat on her husband, or skip work. Eventually that got old, and me not having a phone affected her conscience, whereas I had no conscience– I was single, Irish, unemployed, happy, handsome, the American Dream!

Unemployment was fucking amazing. The amount of strangeness that had gravitated my way over the years was on overtime because I was home all the time, and the ladies knew I was home, had no girlfriend, and I was happier than ever. I love this fucking country!

Miranda warned me that Barkley was going to try and rehire me. Barkley, now nervous and desperate to hold onto his business, emailed me at my AOL address a few times to rehire me, which I wouldn't see until Aunt Mammy and Uncle Liam let me use their 56k internets. His desperate demands to get ahold of me were laughable. Miranda had not warned him of my newfound religion, which was being an asshole to American douchebags.

I declined all of his rehiring offers. I mentioned to him that I would consider an offer if he guaranteed me a six figure salary with my own closed door office, a bed in case I need a nap, my own lock and key, an aquarium, and a waterfall with no windows on the walls (the outside world of Rockford is not pretty), two desks– one for an evil computer, and the other for illustrations and writing, music, etc.–a surround sound system for my records, and no telephones. No phones are allowed in my presence.

Other demands such as, "I don't do meetings on Mondays or Fridays... I must be left alone between the hours of 9am and 4pm on the other days... I don't work past 5pm, ever, and someone else gets the overnight deadlines– not me... I am not your slave, Irish, peasant boy anymore.... Also, I get 3 months of paid vacation days a year that I can use whenever and without approval... Lastly, Miranda gets to be my personal assistant."

He said there was no way in hell he could agree to those demands.

I provided closure once and for all: "Barkley, there is no way in hell I could ever work again for an American douchebag whose only talent in life was inheriting someone else's money. Good luck to you. You're going to get everything you deserve without my help."

And he did.

Barkley's business went bankrupt by 2011– sadly, he still owes me a few thousand dollars for contracted work I agreed to produce on my terms. Terms that he still abused.

Once an American $cumbag, always a douchebag.

(Chapters 18-36 to be continued in another book... Or never.)

Pizzas For Ponies

I am your Bruce Springsteen Junior Jr., baby
I make the pizzas for the ponies, oh oh oh oh oh oh oh oh
I am the boss, Rayrayrayrayrayrayrayray
Bah bah bah bah bah bah bah bah
We will ride this horse into the oven
Picking up pizzas, feeee-e-e-eeeed the ponies
Ha ha ha ha ha hot. burn their tongues
Burn the ponies tongues!
Burn the ponies tongues!
Pizza for ponies I am the boss, baby
Pizza for ponies I am the boss, baby
Pizza for ponies I am the boss, baby
Bah bah bah bah bah bah bah bah
oh oh oh oh oh oh oh oh
I am your Bruce Springsteen Junior Jr., baby
I make pizzas for ponies

Irish Brian Kelly: Poet, Engineer, Landscaper, Lover

#Potato skin Recipe.

I need:

1. Potato
2. Knife
3. Hands
4. Pot
5. Fire
6. Water
7. Salt
8. Butter
9. Bacon
10. Cheese
11. #Pizza
12. italian nachos
13. mexican strombolis
14. phone camera
15. hashtags
16. fake friends
17. BroadBand speed

Directions:

a. Bake on high for INTURONET
b. #blessed | r u #grateful
c. Give no fucks   d. YOU$A™

I Mash Potatoes On My Face, What You Do Today?

Go go go, Bono, goal!!!

Irish Brian Kelly: *Poet, Engineer, Landscaper, Lover*

I Meet Dirty Rockfird Lady, Now I Need More Irish Spring Soap

i had good life in dublin
i make ok life in belvidere
i meet dirty lady in rockfird

now i need more irish spring soap

my life stinks
take me home to dublin
rockfird iz trying to kill me

now i need more irish spring soap

when u aint got nothing
(and u smell like dirty rockfird lady)
u ain't got nothing to lose

now i need more irish spring soap

Ray Tarte's Last High Coups

You, my drunk rabbit;
share, like, enjoy this carrot.
Pizza crust burns slow.

And so he pondered the alternative before deleting himself.

You, my drunk rabbit;
share, like, enjoy this carrot.
Thesis soul craysee.

Ponies Go Poopy High Coup Coo

Oh hi, Jay. 'Sup, Mark?!
Ponies Farting In Rhythm
Return to Sender

Live Like Lobster, Die Like Truck

Live like lobster die
like truck; ha ha ha ha ha.
Sublimation blues.

Irish Brian Kelly: *Poet, Engineer, Landscaper, Lover*

Same Game, Different Name

Oh, poor, poor Aaron!
Phillipe, Danny, Mark, Andy, Dave, Chris.
Houses fixed, stacked cards.

I Mash Potatoes On My Face, What You Do Today?

Squirting Soap

#gratefullly resigned
deploring reality
squirting soap remains

Irish Brian Kelly: *Poet, Engineer, Landscaper, Lover*

CASINOS AND TRAINS
POTATOES AND SOUPS

CASINOS AND TRAINS
POTATOES AND SOUPS
WHERE HAS THE TIME GONE?
NOW I GO POOPS

I Mash Potatoes On My Face, What You Do Today?

i <3 #doughnuts

i make u donuts
donuts r good 4 me
donuts r good 4 u
u and me eat donuts
i lick u
u lick me
we eat donuts
we r donuts
if we could b donuts
i heart <3 emoji u
#doughnuts
lol

Irish Brian Kelly: *Poet, Engineer, Landscaper, Lover*

I MAKE MASHED POTATO CAKE ON YOUR FACE

I MAKE MASHED POTATOES CAKE ON YOUR FACE

HAHAHA

NOW I EAT YOUR FACE

MASHED POTATOES CAKE ON YOUR FACE, BABY!

HAPPY BIRTHDAY, BABY, I MAKE YOU DAY OLD POTATO PEEL CAKE

IF TODAY ES YOUR BIRTHDAY
I MAKE YOU DAY OLD POTATO PEEL CAKE
YOU SHARE ET WITH INTERNET
THEY SAY, "THANK YOU, IRISH BRIAN!"
I SAY, "HAPPY BIRTHDAY, YOU EAT DAY OLD POTATO PEEL CAKE, BABY!"
HAHAHAHAHA

Number 138:
POTATOES ON YOUR FACE GO POW POW POW

I MIGHT SEEM LIKE A REAL DUMB MOTHERFUCKER, but truth of the matter is that my IQ was last tested with the WAIS (Weschler) scale around 138. Anyone who has a fucking clue about IQ scores will tell you I'm borderline brilliant, if not a genius. I am neither. I am a goddamned Irish asshole who wants to waste your time on the internets.

It's true, I choose to type in all-caps and say stupid fucking things because I can, will and you can't, don't. Most of you are goddamned American amateurs regardless of IQ scores and all-caps buttons, because you choose to be inspired by shitty music, books, film, politics and false prophets.

(The fourth wall remains cracked for now, small caps continued.)

Typically a higher IQ means I would have had a higher chance at being a somewhat successful doctor, scientist, etcetera, instead of what I am: Irish Brian Kelly. Poet, engineer and landscaper. However, that is not the case. I am a product of my environment, Dublin, Ireland, and Belvedere, IL. Each environment I call "home" has been infected by class warfare, corruption and economic imbalance.

With regards to IQ scores, environment and genetics has much to do with IQ scores and opportunities to succeed. I can offer you this as living proof: I am one smart mother fucker who has had to fight through dealing with poor opportunity-less surroundings and the system to succeed every step of the way, because the system of authority is stacked with overly proud, stupid ass, privileged mother fuckers who possess lower IQs, money and power.

Money and power matters more than intelligence when it comes to influencing herds of people, societies and countries. Civilization is defined and rewarded by ownership, having more, building more, buying more– not intellect. Having more intellect than the herd simply means you're more likely to jump off a cliff to be with like minds if you're environment is consistently parented, taught, governed, supervised and policed by goddamned amateurs.

Therefor, I recognized my fate early on while being labeled as brilliant and borderline genius material. I am poor by choice and choose not to give a fuck because it's funnier. Laughing is healthier. Challenging you goddamned amateurs on a daily basis to give less shits about your digital existence is more important to me than publishing the report I've worked 23 years on.

A report that time and lesser hydro-fueled minds has caught up with that will revolutionize the auto, aviation and oil industries. I would be killed for publishing my findings, so I won't. I'd rather live, laugh and mash my fucking potatoes on your goddamned face.

FEEL IT. TOUCH YOUR TABLET.
FEEL YOUR PHONE.
POTATOES ON YOUR FACE GO POW POW POW
MASH IT UP, BABY, YUM!
HAHAHA

Irish Brian Kelly: *Poet, Engineer, Landscaper, Lover*

HUMPTY DUMPTY DAY POTATO

HUMPTY DUMPTY SAT ON A POTATO
HUMPTY DUMPTY MASHED ON HIS BUTT
TODAY THE HUMPTY TOMORROW THE HUMP
LICKETY SPLIFITY POTATO DA BUTT
TICKLE THE PEACHES AND MASHUH DA POTATOES
DO IT WITH YOUR TONGUE AND MASH IT WITH YOUR BUTT
ADD A BANANA AND SAY WHAT THE F*CK?!
HAHAHA

HIGH COUP #298: CAREFUL THOUGHTS OF YOUS, HAHAHA

PANTS DROPPED AT THE KNEES
MORNING MOVEMENTS ARRIVE, BREATHE;
CAREFUL THOUGHTS OF YOUS

I BILL YOU AND MASH TATOES ON YOUR FACE

Dear _____
(Insert any name of any pony's face to mash a potato with),

Tell me what to do:
I bill you and mash the potatoes on your face.

Tell me what I can and can't do without me asking for it, nor you paying for it, and:
I bill you and then come up with a new cartoon name for you before I mash another potato on your face. Example: Mister Meerasaké, Jay The Pony, and more.

Tell me what you think I should be doing with my time, and:
I bill you again with new fees. Then I draw a character cartoon to match your new cartoon name while treating all forms of communication with you as a joke, along with mashing a few more potatoes on your face.

Talk about me to people that you know who will tell me after you realize I'm treating you in return with the same amount of disrespect that you've handed to me to begin with, and:
I bill you with additional fees, draw more cartoons with you new name, and give you a Facebook page. #lol = laughs out louds.

Oh yeah, don't forget:
I mash a dozen more TATOES on your face, and on your Facebook cartoon page.

Talk about me to strangers in bars who end up finding me on the internet to tell me, and:
I bill you with new fees, including late past due invoice(s) fees and legal fees, along with drawing more cartoons that comprise a storybook collection in your new name to share on your Facebook fan page with a big burlap bag of potatoes to mash on your face. Then, I publish a book with your cartoon name to thank you for being an American douchebag.

Keep talking and I will bill, illustrate, and write out the end of our story for you on my terms with endless bags of potatoes mashed on your face. Our stories have no endings, guaranteed to last until I die.

Should you choose to strangely respect me for once, I respect you– however, the few of you who chose to burn me have no penance coming your way. Disrespect me and I mash the potatoes on your fucking face. (LOL = #laughsoutlouds)

Pay your bills and I won't mash potatoes on your face. That's how a healthy balance in Irish Brian's universe works.

I Before E

Everyone laughed when I said, "I don't like babies."
I wasn't joking.
Everyone laughed when I said, "Real estate is for sinners."
I wasn't joking.
Everyone laughed when I said, "Four point eight out of five teachers are idiots."
I wasn't joking.
Everyone laughed when I misspelled "weird" on purpose.
I wasn't joking.
Everyone laughed and called me weird, but I didn't laugh.
I wasn't joking.

I think you're all a bunch of selfish, all-knowing, greedy, materialistic, privileged American assholes and sluts.

"Why are you so angry?" I am not angry.

The truth is as it appears: I'm not who you want me to be.
I can not pretend to be anything other than the son of a poor immigrant.
I am Irish Brian Kelly, and you are not.
You are an American.
You will never know what it's like to see through everyone and everything from the outside.

"i" before "e" except after "c" and in the case of "weird"

Love Is A Fatal American Expense

Once I was a young Irish man with a used couch and a 13" TV that I bought in 1997. I slept on the floor with a pillow and thought nothing strange of it before I owned a used couch. My closest friends would stop by and worry, but whatever. I am a man of few needs, and having a couch is an American luxury for a boy from Ireland.

The couch came to me (after the last of my mother's parents passed away) with plastic vinyl covering its entirety. No one had ever sat on it; it being on display in their living room for much of the 20 years my grandparents had it. I tore off the plastic vinyl protective cover once it was in my possession to sleep on.

I was happy and hard working with no bad debts tied to my name, except for the student loans– good debts they used to be as some American economists have been known to say on the 13" TV and in financial planning books. Irish Brian Kelly begs to differ.

While most of my peers were boozing it up, getting married and making babies, I chose to work more. I started my own business– actually, I was forced into figuring out how to start my own business to survive in America. After working many years for privileged American idiots, I had no other choice to survive than to work for myself.

Dating and settling down like many do in their 20s and early 30s wasn't a financial option to consider with my American experience. Women knocking on my door, calling me–bootie calls as the Americans called them–became overwhelmingly annoying. I had many options, but I did not want a lady in my life to suck the remains of my creative energy away from work. Irish work ethics was going to pay the bills, not American lady friends.

Don't misunderstand my sexuality as many did–I love ladies, and my beer can cock shot up to the sky at least one to 1400 times a day thinking about one or two of those fine bootie calls–but it was nothing that my hands couldn't comply with to satisfy healthy urges when presented. Costs less, too.

I saw dating as an American luxury, an expense that I couldn't afford. I couldn't afford to buy Chili's Restaurant meals for someone else, go to the movies, and all that jazz that leads to sloppy protected sex, romance, love making, LOLs, more dinners, trips away, engagements, and incredibly uninspiring life planning for events such as weddings, real estate, insurances, and suicides. Unprotected sex to make another human being eventually becomes a life event. Another expense I could never afford. A free, used couch and a 13" TV fit into my budget. I knew my limitations.

Work was going well by 2003, or so I thought, so I upgraded to a 28" tube Panasonic TV vs. considering the multiple expenses that comes along with investing in dating. The 28" TV was cheaper and had an on/off power button along with a volume up/down and mute option that I could manage and be responsible for without ever having to feel guilty.

There is no way to tell a lady to be quiet when she needs to share her feelings and you're not into it. The TV was cheaper, plus it allowed me to save more money for a rainy day someday– a few rainy days would arrive because of the expense of dating.

I met my first American wife in 2005, we dated. It was a luxury, but not romance.

I Mash Potatoes On My Face, What You Do Today?

Part of me gave up is how I see these few, fatal, decision making mistakes now. Tired of answering questions from friends and family back home in Dublin such as, "Aren't you worried about dying alone?" and "Don't you want to have kids someday?" No and no were easy, confident answers.

Everyone thought I was depressed and opted for easy nos, but I wasn't depressed. I was happy and using my Irish brain, being responsible and knowing my financial limitations. (What's right for me doesn't have to be right for the rest of you fucking assholes. Respect my rights, I respect yours.)

Feeling pressure to "grow up," I invested greatly in this American dating-expense risk in 2005 and 2006, and we were married by 2007. She had robbed me blind by 2008 in so many ways that it has taken me years to piece together this evil American lady's incredibly well thought-out financial heists.

Lies that ranged in scope: Like showing up to a closing on an American home purchase that I made at her insistence/begging with the $0 she contributed. $0 left over from a $40,000 lawsuit she supposedly won in 2006, that she lived off of for months without a job while house hunting for her first property.

A plan of hers that I had originally removed myself from until the wheels fell off her wagon, and lies piled up to fool me even further into buying a home for us while we were engaged– because no bank and mortgage loan lender wanted to work with her. Using my credit, as she had none, and using my savings, as she had none as well to contribute, I was fooled into a real estate investment.

What happened to that little American real estate investment is a book in itself. The amount of people she has conned along the way have their own stories about this lady. Oh, fuck me, I'm being too kind– a snake. She fooled many along the way with small and large heists.

E.g., a small heist: The birthday gift iPod. She took money from friends and family to buy me a birthday gift in late 2007. She charged it to my American store credit card instead, and used the $400 plus in cash that she took from friends and family to 'buy thanksgiving dinner for her family' as she put it to me months later.

Truth is, she blew the cash in bars with her boyfriends, one of them she was already cheating on with only a few months after being married. My Irish ass never saw it coming. She loved being in bars with boys so much that she ended up working in a few bars, too– to con other future boyfriends she could line up behind whoever she was cheating on. Property owners she could con, and so many more that it takes its own book to process. Her life and lies are a book with a trail of people like me that she has fooled, abused, and robbed from.

I paid my American store credit card for the iPod, my birthday gift from everyone closest to me, after our divorce in 2008. A small example of trust abused on a small heist to acquire $400 plus from my friends and family. Now imagine the larger things this snake of a person pulled off. I'm still legally dealing with all of it.

The signs were in front of me to not invest in dating this snake, but I used my heart instead of my brain to allow trust to be abused. My brain kept screaming at me, "Bollocks! Wake up! Why are you marrying this snake?

I Mash Potatoes On My Face, What You Do Today?

You are too smart for marriage."

That trust which was abused by my first wife extended itself to my hard earned savings, my hard work, my name in the community, my sisters, my parents, and my friends. Many so-called friends, who I have no shame in calling foolish backstabbing ponies today, are not allowed in my presence anymore.

I lost everything one could work hard for in this country because of one, evil American. My work, reputation, trust in others, savings, credit, and abilities to try harder had been tainted by one fatal, financial mistake– to date an evil, fucking snake.

Nothing has gone right since allowing evil in my presence despite major successes to sever snakes from my adopted life. Anything one could ever want to work hard for has backfired in mysterious medical ways. Giving into the wonder, the sadness, and the randomness of all this life stuff keeps me focused. However, there are darker moments.

I've accidentally come to understand why people kill themselves off to be anyone other than who they were born as. There is a frightful, calming, selfish peace combined with helplessness that creeps in every now and then. I miss my homeland, Ireland, and I don't want to live in America anymore. This peaceful, helpless feeling began in 1987 to be exact. That's the first time I remember sadness affecting me in a way that I felt numb, disabled, damaged and done for. I was a kid keep in mind. All I wanted to do was to be someone else when it occurred.

"Get me out of this fucking head. I am Irish Brian. Why am I in America?

What is this dream that Pappy and Mammy talk about? Blimey potatoes."

That feeling came back more and more over the years as I adjusted myself to the American life. It would pick up steam, week on/week off battles. There are months that it disappears, and I don't know why. Out of the blue, something triggers it– anything, the sun, a snowstorm, a grocery store line, a green beer on March 17th, the cry of a fake irishman's praise–St. Patty wasn't even Irish, you dumb Americans–and there it is creeping in like a snake asking to have its head severed and replaced by something calm and peaceful.

It's the reoccurrence of this feeling that worries me the most, because no one I know would understand how comfortable these Irish ideas become. Try to process the idea of leaving this beautiful planet. Those with serious addictions must be weaker to its deceptive lure, the peacefulness, because I can barely tolerate an emotional low from taking any over the counter headache and allergy pills.

I often wonder: What if I didn't have the power of the pen, ink, pencil, paper, guitar, piano, and Irish Brian? What if I didn't have an imagination or the physical abilities to use it? What if I could wake up and actually mash a fucking potato on my face to feel better?

I had the secret to life figured out, happiness was simple to achieve, and all it took was owning an abundance of loneliness, a 13" TV, a used couch, and a lack of material possessions. I was living proof of the new American Dream, Irish Brian Kelly.

I Mash Potatoes On My Face, What You Do Today?

I miss that old couch and 13″ TV, but more importantly, I miss Dublin. The ladies use soap, the men use toilet paper, the beer is real (not green and watered down), luck isn't related to hard work, and lastly, love is affordable.

Love is a fatal American expense.

Taters GONNA TATE

Irish Brian Kelly: *Poet, Engineer, Landscaper, Lover*

Are you uncomfortable yet? (Part 2)

fourth wall destroyed, pause
readers ponder final scene
go go go, bono

I Can't Afford to Die Here

Property taxes, yards, insurances, investments, tithing, retirement.
I can't take it anymore.

The last warning:
I don't want what the goddamn American amateurs have.
Albeit, good for them.

They have a boat and pension;
I wrote this book.
#LOL

They bought bigger homes;
I recorded a record.
#LOL

Do whatever you please to,
and most of you will anyway without taking this warning into account,
but I can't afford to die here.

Irish Brian Kelly: *Poet, Engineer, Landscaper, Lover*

The Rabbit's Hole

The rabbit's hole has many layers
Try and fail, you will, Yoda, you will
You are not the carrot, nor its roots
Not even a little bunny becomes you
Hop along, mother fuckers, hop along
Make like a pony, hum like a hornet
Mimic, mock, and belittle
but another garden blooms, not you
No, not you, little pony
potato peeling peasant
shit shoveling $cumbag
the list is long with names to appetize
I am the goddamn bunny and the carrot
shovel it or eat it, the hole is waiting
Fucking amateurs
#laughsoutlouds = lol

I Mash Potatoes On My Face, What You Do Today?

Thank you
Jay, Mark, Cory,
Heather, PNC Bank, McHenry County,
Winnebago County, Frank, Don, Sparky,
Gordon, Jarrod, Britney, Tim, Bono,
Larry, Adam, Edge, David Gray,
Damien Rice, Quarry Shazzelle, Saint
Palladius and anyone else I may have
Forgotten

Potatoes.

Tom Stotes and The True Story of Low Hanging Fruits

This is a true story. I misspelled Tom's last name to protect his identity. Actually, I misspelled the last name to protect one of the few holes he puts in his pants, the asshole. LOL.

I don't know Tom, let's get that out of the way first.

I met him at a Compact Disc (CD) Mix Exchange Dinner Party in 2006. Patrick and Anita's house on the corner of Ridge and Yonge streets in Rockford, IL. I thought nothing of the American douchebag at that time. Was introduced to him–as I was to many people that night–and shook his hand, ate some chips and dip, opted for the bacon wrapped hot dog bits, life goes on. I attended a few CD exchange parties at Patrick and Anita's over the years and they were always fun, always meeting new people.

Skip forward to 2009. I receive a call from my friend, Zak, who says, "I was showing a few people your RockfordSymbol.com site at the bar, laughing, except for one person in this group– Tom Stotes. Do you know him by chance?"

"No, I do not know Tom Stotes... May have met a guy by that name once at a party? Don't know, why?" I say.

"He had a meltdown at the bar like he may have something against you and says, "That's not funny. He's not funny. I don't get it that guy. Not funny– low hanging fruit. That there is low hanging fruit."

I Mash Potatoes On My Face, What You Do Today?

I laugh for a bit and ask Zak a few questions. "Wait, who's this guy?!" and "What was his problem exactly?"

"Low hanging fruit. He thinks everything you do is low hanging fruit, particularly RockfordSymbol.com," confirms Zak.

I laugh, "Huh, that's weird. I don't know this guy."

We laugh more. Zak says, "Apparently he knows who you are and doesn't like anything you do which is funny. The comedian who doesn't like you."

Now, people, I don't know who Tom Stotes is. I don't know his story, and I couldn't point that proud, condescending Rockford fuck out of a fast food line.

I get curious because that's what I do, and I dig a bit for information on Tom Stotes. "Who is this funny guy?" I'm thinking.

There he is, on the Facebook dot com. I recognized him. All I could think was, "Wow. It's that fat comedian guy I met at the CD exchange party in 2006. This guy hates me? What did I do to him? What the fuck– and he's a comedian... Ahahahhaha!" Yes.

I couldn't stop laughing at the fact that a comedian–a self-proclaimed one–had it out for me, and I had no idea why.

So, in honor of Tom Stotes' critique of me and my work, I created a special gallery of work in late 2009: 18 new illustrations simply titled, "Low Hanging Fruits and Vegetables," in honor of Tom Stotes.

There hung 18 shitty illustrations of fruits and vegetables. A banana, apple, orange, peas, grapes, potato, tomato, red pepper and much more. All in honor of that fat, proud fuck I met once, shook his hand, and then saw on the facebook after he did some 1974 ABA trash talking, Tom Stotes.

Remember, I don't know the guy and still think nothing of it aside from creating a series of shitty illustrations inspired, of course, by his shitty existence and critique of me.

Skip forward to early 2011.

A friend of mine, Zach (note, not the same Zak as previously mentioned before), is working with a start-up comedy improv group called, "Free Kittens." He and his peers ask me to illustrate a logo for them, and if there's time a poster design to help launch their collective. I do such.

The improv conducts their first board meeting, which I am not invited to attend, and my logo ideas are presented. Lo and behold, Tom Stotes is a member of their board. Chaos ensues once my name and work is mentioned for approval.

To paraphrase Tom Stotes: "Fuck that guy. No way. I refuse to allow his participation in this improv. I'll come up with something better."

A discussion ensues, with me not there remember, as to why Tom Stotes has it out for me. No real answer is given, but those who witness it can't feel anything but humor, and can't wait to call me the moment their first meeting break commences.

I Mash Potatoes On My Face, What You Do Today?

"Brian, you're not going to believe this," says Zach on the other end of the line, during a gray, mid-Saturday afternoon. "I'm at this comedy improv meeting, our first board meeting, and we spent the last 10 minutes before this break arguing about you. A bunch of local comedians arguing about your logo, poster, and you. It was so funny. A few of us couldn't stop laughing at the irony of it all because you're not here, and here we are, a bunch of amateur comedians arguing about you. Ahahhahahahaha."

I laugh, Zach laughs, I ask some questions:

"Who was arguing? What did I do? What the fuck?"

"Tom Stotes, man! That guy really hates you is all I can gather, or he hates your illustration style. We don't know! It was funny, though– the irony of an angry local comedian who really didn't know that many of us know you and found the whole thing funny. I wish you were here to laugh at all of this. This is crazy."

I laughed, Zach laughed, conversation over.

Problem is, a few more local comedians called me to talk about Tom Stotes' meltdown at the comedy improv meeting. I got the point. Another random local loser had it out for me.

Problem remains: I don't know this fucking guy. I don't have time to. I'm obviously doing something right, or wrong enough, to have the attention of a wannabe comedian, artist, and fast food afficionado.

I decided to hold off on creating a new series of illustrative work in honor of Tom Stotes' bizarre behavior by opting to include his story in this book years later. I don't believe in the high road, or silence, or do unto others as you would want them to shit on you; no, I believe in taking the road to retribution– and mashing potatoes on mother fucking American faces.

That's right– YOU$A™!

I want all Tom Stotes wannabes to know that I will honor and remember you one way or another, years and decades later, if you fuck with me, and my friends and family in unwarranted, unkind ways. I have no qualms about going to hell for telling you to go fuck yourselves off my way with a meandering story like this in a book. This book.

Little ponies fenda outrun the master horsey, but end up with a bag of potatoes mashed on their faces.

Later, Tater Tots.

I Mash Potatoes On My Face, What You Do Today?

I took a potato, held it in front of my face, stared at it, thought of all of you and called it out by your names. One by one I mashed that Tatoe on my face!

I licked my lips when I was done mashing my face with the potato and thought, "Hmm, that could use some cheese, bacon, and butter.
Hold the salt, lady."

Listen here, American douchebag bubbas: Next time you attempt to burn someone like Irish Brian Kelly, insure that you blow this potato peeling, cornbeef eating, cheap beer drinking, motherfucker up!

Until then, may you all mash a big ol' burlap bag of fat, rock-hard potatoes on your slimy, snake-skinned faces. That's right, YOU$A!™

Go go go, Bono, goal!

Irish Brian Kelly
Poet, Engineer, Landscaper, Lover

www.ingramcontent.com/pod-product-compliance
Lightning Source LLC
Chambersburg PA
CBHW030625230426
43661CB00053B/2150